FOUND IN TRANSLATION

Volume 2

❖

RHONDA K. KINDIG

WESTBOW°
PRESS
A DIVISION OF THOMAS NELSON
& ZONDERVAN

Scripture taken from the New Revised Standard Version Bible, copyright 1989, Division of Christian Education of the National Council of Churches of Christ in the United States of America. Used by permission. All rights reserved.

WestBow Press books may be ordered through booksellers or by contacting:

WestBow Press
A Division of Thomas Nelson & Zondervan
1663 Liberty Drive
Bloomington, IN 47403
www.westbowpress.com
1 (866) 928-1240

Because of the dynamic nature of the Internet, any web addresses or links contained in this book may have changed since publication and may no longer be valid. The views expressed in this work are solely those of the author and do not necessarily reflect the views of the publisher, and the publisher hereby disclaims any responsibility for them.

Any people depicted in stock imagery provided by Thinkstock are models, and such images are being used for illustrative purposes only. Certain stock imagery © Thinkstock.

ISBN: 978-1-4908-8293-2 (sc)

Library of Congress Control Number: 2011928732

Print information available on the last page.

WestBow Press rev. date: 07/28/2015

DEDICATION

+For the ecumenical women of
UPPER ROOM

and

+For the St Thomas
GUARDIANS of the **WORD**

Thanks be to God!

Table of Contents

FOREWORD
By Pastor James H. Bangle

Barely three verses into Genesis, God speaks a simple word, *Light!* And things begin to happen. Big things. With a creative word, scripture introduces us to the power of words. Deeper study tells us that *"Light"* actually has the nuance of *to enlighten.* As a gifted scholar, teacher, and person of faith, Rhonda Kindig invites us to see the Word through words and to become exposed to its light. In this book she guides readers into themes of the Old Testament with a style that is both educational and devotional and helps us see the Hebrew Scriptures in a new light. Her fondness for words and their power to enlighten and change our lives shines through.

This volume is the complement to Kindig's, *Found in Translation*, in which she takes a similar approach to New Testament words. We are fortunate have her insights. The words of Isaiah are fitting:

"The Lord God has given me
the tongue of a teacher,
that I may know how to sustain
the weary with a word.
Morning by morning he wakens —
wakens my ear
to listen as those who are taught."
Isaiah 50:4

James H. Bangle, Pastor

Translation Note

All of the scriptural references in this text are taken from the **New Revised Standard Version** of the Holy Bible. The essays on the vocabulary are, therefore, based upon the English vocabulary choices used within the New Revised Standard Version (NRSV). The NRSV is the Bible translation currently in use in the Revised Common Lectionary followed by the Lutheran and Episcopal churches in this country. If you use a different Bible translation, some of the statements in these essays may disagree with word choices from your particular translation.

Preface

For folks who enjoy digging deeper into Bible stories to find recurring themes, I hope the collection of short essays in this volume will meet your expectations.

For people curious about vocabulary choices and alternate translation possibilities, I hope this volume will satisfy your questions.

For those who thought the first volume, <u>Found in Translation</u>, was a helpful resource for approaching the New Testament through Greek word choices, I hope Volume 2 will enable you to similarly explore, via Hebrew vocabulary, the Old Testament themes, which are foundational to New Testament understanding.

For anyone seeking a new way to "keep" Lent, the essays function ideally as devotionals for both study and reflection. I hope this volume will be just what you need. Though it is not necessary to save this volume for a Lenten discipline, if you wish to do so, a structure for matching the days in Lent with the contents may be found in the appendix.

I am pleased to share what I have found in translation.

Thanks be to God!
Rhonda K. Kindig

Very Quick Summary of Books of Bible

Hebrew Bible (Christian Old Testament)

Genesis—tales of creation, Noah & flood; patriarchal history Abraham's family

Exodus—Moses leads Israelites out of bondage in Egypt to Mt Sinai; commandments

Leviticus—legal codes

Numbers—Moses' leadership continues in wilderness sojourn

Deuteronomy—retelling of story of Moses

Joshua—conquest of Canaan

Judges—period of time before monarchy when local leaders ruled

Ruth—faithful foreigner becomes great grandmother of King David

1 & 2 Samuel—man of God, Samuel, anoints first two kings, Saul then David

1 & 2 Kings—King Solomon and subsequent kings of Israel and Judah, prophet Elijah

1 & 2 Chronicles—retelling of history of kings, ending with fall of Jerusalem

Ezra & Nehemiah—return after Exile in Babylon, rebuilding the Temple

Esther—Hebrew Queen in Persia saves her people (explains Purim)

Job—man who suffers great hardship questions God's justice

Psalms—collection of hymns

Proverbs—pithy sayings about life

Ecclesiastes—musings about life by a preacher

Song of Solomon—love poem

Isaiah—prophetic writings of exhortation and encouragement, Messianic texts

Jeremiah—prophetic writings of exhortation and encouragement

Lamentations—attributed to Jeremiah

Ezekiel—while in Exile, Ezekiel envisions God's new plan

Daniel—apocalyptic vision—keep the faith while in Exile

Hosea, Joel, Amos, Obadiah, Jonah, Micah, Nahum, Habakkuk, Zephaniah, Haggai, Zechariah, and Malachi—twelve minor prophets writing before, during, and after the Exile, with words of exhortation and encouragement

Continued

8

New Testament

Matthew, Mark, Luke—gospel accounts of the ministry and passion story of Jesus

John—gospel with a different focus on the ministry and passion story of Jesus

Acts of the Apostles—stories of apostles, especially Peter, then Paul

Romans, 1 & 2 Corinthians, Galatians, Ephesians, Philippians, Colossians, 1 & 2 Thessalonians, 1 & 2 Timothy, Titus, Philemon, Hebrews, James, 1 & 2 Peter, 1,2,3 John, and Jude—all are letters to or from apostles, many from Paul

Revelation—apocalyptic vision that asks—whom do you worship when oppressed?

Very Quick Timeline of Bible Times

@3000 *BC(BCE)*	Sumerian Culture—earliest known writing
1450 *or* 1250	Exodus from Egypt
1200 – 1025	Israel emerges in Canaan
1025 – 1005	Saul is King of Israel
1005 – 965	David is King of Israel
968 – 928	Solomon is King of Israel
928 +	Monarchy is divided: Israel in north; Judah in south
722	Assyria conquers Samaria (northern kingdom)—ten northern tribes "lost"
586	Babylon captures Jerusalem; Temple destroyed—deportation/exile to Babylon
538	King Cyrus II of Persia allows return of exiles
445 – 430	Nehemiah is governor of Judah; Temple rebuilt
336 – 323	Alexander the Great
49 – 44	Julius Caesar
37 – 4	Herod the Great rebuilds Second Temple
70 *AD(CE)*	Rome destroys Second Temple

In the Beginning

"In the day that the LORD God made the earth and the heavens, when no plant of the field was yet in the earth and no herb of the field had yet sprung up—for the LORD God had not caused it to rain upon the earth, and there was no one to till the ground; but a stream would rise from the earth, and water the whole face of the ground—then the LORD God formed man from the dust of the ground, and breathed into his nostrils the breath of life; and the man became a living being. And the LORD God planted a garden in Eden, in the east; and there he put the man whom he had formed." Genesis 2:4-8

Whenever folks first begin Bible studies of Genesis, they are often surprised that there are two distinct stories of creation—each with a different chronology. Check it out: Genesis 1:1-2:3 is the majestic, poetic story most of us know, right? What day do plants appear? Day 3, before the humans show up. Okay, now check out Genesis 2:4-9. When do the plants appear in this version? *After* the man has been formed!

You'll notice another difference, too. In chapter 1, God is called "God", but in chapter 2, God is "LORD God". It is an established teaching that two separate sources supplied these differing narratives. These were later interwoven into one text. As you read the Bible, you may notice other stories appear more than once with slightly differing details or names.

There are other divergences in the creation accounts. The next question for you: Was the man created before the woman? In the first story, "male and female" ("humankind") are created at the same moment in time, both in the image of God (Gen. 1:27).

The second story requires us to know some Hebrew. In chapter 2, man is the Hebrew **adam**, meaning an "earth creature", without gender. The *adam* is made from the imprint of God from the **adamah**, which is the "ground". Not until verse 22 does God separate this earthling into two distinct genders, **ishshah** and **ish** (female and male). It is at this point that we read the first human words recorded in the Bible—and it is a love song about the woman from the man!

Sometimes we tend to be stuck with preconceived notions about these Bible stories going way back to our childhood Sunday school days. Discussing the stories with others can lead us to fresh perspectives and understandings. Thanks be to God!

"Thus the heavens and the earth were finished, and all their multitude. And on the seventh day God finished the work that he had done, and he rested on the seventh day from all the work that he had done. So God blessed the seventh day and hallowed it, because on it God rested from all the work that he had done in creation." Genesis 2:1-3

The Breath of Life

"In the beginning when God created the heavens and earth, the earth was a formless void and darkness covered the face of the deep, while a wind from God swept over the face of the waters." Genesis 1:1-2

"Then the LORD God formed man from the dust of the ground and breathed into his nostrils the breath of life; and the man became a living being." Genesis 2:7

We are intimately familiar with the "breath of life", but have you given much thought to this breath that sustains us with every inhalation? It was also there "in the beginning" sweeping over the deep, because it is the same Hebrew word, **ruah**, in both verses.

Try this experiment right now: cup your hand directly in front of your mouth and speak aloud the word *ruah*. Did you feel it?

Ruah, the very breath God exhales, is the wind through the atmosphere, if we read these verses literally. Also in Genesis (8:1) this is the wind that dries up the flood waters witnessed by Noah. In Exodus 14:21-22, this is the wind that separates the waters of the sea. In 1 Kings 19:11-12, this is the wind that Elijah hears.

This is also the breath that Jesus breathes upon his disciples in John 20:22, thereby giving them the Holy Spirit. Yes, *ruah* may also be translated as "spirit". [In John, of course, the original word is the Greek **pneuma**; the same word that is the stem for *pneumatic, which means air-driven.*]

Look for this *ruah*; listen for this *pneuma*. The creation story tells us the *ruah* "swept" over the water. An alternate translation reads the *ruah* "hovered" over the water! Just as the *pneuma* (Spirit), which is the same *ruah*, the creative, life-giving breath of God, "hovered" over Jesus like a dove would have done and then descended and alighted upon him at his baptism (Matthew 3:16). Just as the *pneuma* rushed like a "violent wind" filling the disciples at Pentecost (Acts 2:2)

We also find the Spirit (the same *ruah*, the same *pneuma*) as the root of the word *inspiration*. Many people say the Bible is the "inspired word of God". What does this mean? It is in and through encounters with this word that we are the ones inspired.

"But truly it is the spirit in a mortal,
the breath of the Almighty,
that makes for understanding." Job 32:8

"When you send forth your spirit [breath] they are created." Psalm 104:30

In His Image

"So God created humankind in his image,
in the image of God he created them;
male and female he created them." Genesis 1:27

We have all used the idiom before: "He's the spitting image of his father." To us, this use means that when we look upon the child, we can see the physical likeness to the parent. In fact, we are so accustomed to this usage, we probably assume that is what the creation story of the first chapter of Genesis is also saying. What do you believe?

Actually there has never been consensus among church folk for what "in his image" truly means. There has been endless speculation about whether Genesis 1:27 is suggesting a mirror-like reflection of physical likeness or not.

The English word "image" is the translation of the Hebrew word **tselem**, a word that denotes a shadow, a copy, or even a counterpart. It can be an outline or a representation of an original. In the political arena, a counterpart or representative stands in or acts on behalf of another. We elect representatives to speak for us in Congress. Ambassadors are appointed to represent us in foreign lands.

Could it be that being in the image of God means that humans are created to act and speak on behalf of the Creator? How is it even possible to reflect the Lordship of God through our actions or our words? We are given clues in the verses that follow the Genesis 1:27 "in his image" passage.

Two possibilities show up in God's instructions to humankind. Genesis 1:28 gives the advice to "be fruitful and multiply". Humans are called to share in creation through procreation. Another clue is in Genesis 2:18-25, when the man is asked to name the animals. Humans are called to share in language from the very One who spoke creation into being.

From there, though, it is up to us. Can we find ways to use these directives, to act and speak on behalf of God in the world? Thanks be to God.

"Whoever sheds the blood of a human,
by a human shall that person's blood be shed;
for in his own image
God made humankind." Genesis 9:6

Subdue It

"Be fruitful and multiply,
and fill the earth and subdue it...
and have dominion* over the fish of the sea
and over the birds of the air
and over every living thing that moves upon the earth." Genesis 1:28

There is a very troubling word in this passage, a word that has caused great concerns over the use and the abuse of all the natural resources of this planet: "subdue". Many individuals, many corporations, many governments have considered this charge of God's to be *carte blanche* given to humans over all of nature. That is, of course, an absurd position.

The Hebrew word translated as "subdue" is **kabash**. If saying that word makes you think of the English word *kibosh*, you would not be too far from the Hebrew definition! One of the ways *kabash* can be translated is "to force" or even "to bring into bondage". So, on the surface, that seems quite harsh.

When trying to figure out appropriate translations for Biblical texts, one of the techniques used is to investigate other uses of the word in the Bible. This very word is also found in Micah 7:19: *He will again have compassion upon us; he will subdue (kabash) our iniquities.*

To try to deduce what the Micah verse is suggesting, it might be very helpful to trace the pedigree of the English word *subdue*. Reaching back through Middle English to Middle French to Old French and then to Latin, we come to the Latin verb *subducere*, which is "to draw away". That works well for the Micah passage. But, for the Genesis use, consider that this Latin verb is intimately related to the Latin verb *seducere,* which is "to seduce".

Now, it seems we might be closer to the intention of the Genesis passage, especially since God's directives to the man about his relationship to the "garden", given just a little later in Genesis 2:15, are *"to tend it and keep it."* The Hebrew for "tend" is **abad**, which can mean "serve" or "worship", while the Hebrew for "keep" is **shamar**, which is to "guard" or "exercise great care over". Neither of these suggests a

17

power-play.   How lovely to think that what humans are called to do with the earth is to lovingly seduce it. Thanks be to God.

"Yet you have made them a little lower than God,
and crowned them with glory and honor.
You have given them dominion
over the works of your hands." Psalm 8:5-6

---

*A further note about *dominion*—
Contrary to popular belief, *dominion* is not related to the word *dominate*. No, it is from the Latin word **dominium**, which is a place where one has settled connections. We are connected to all the creatures of creation; we are not put here to dominate nature!

What Have You Done?

"The man said, 'The woman whom you gave to be with me, she gave me fruit from the tree, and I ate.' Then the LORD God said to the woman, 'What is this that you have done?' The woman said, 'The serpent tricked me, and I ate.'" Genesis 3:12-13

Here is one of those questions that appears about a half dozen times in Genesis, and surely we are meant to hear the echo of the first time it is spoken...which is by God in the garden (Genesis 3:13). Do you ever experiment with inflection when you read—what do you emphasize? *What* have you done? What *have* you done? What have *you* done? What have you *done*? Even then, we may miss nuances of the question. I like to think God's question was not accusatory but rather full of pathos.

The question comes near the conclusion of the "apple" incident...but wait, the word "apple" is never used! (In fact, some Renaissance art shows the Christ child seated on the lap of the Madonna while holding a pomegranate.) What else about this story might we have confused? Can you name the two things "cursed" by God after this act of disobedience?

Many folks believe it is the man and the woman who are cursed by God. Check out Genesis 3:14-19...were you correct? Verses 14-19 are not prescribing punishment at all, instead they are describing consequences. The woman and man have made a choice—a choice of living in the world rather than in paradise, and such a decision will have consequences.

The "labor" of childbirth is the Hebrew word ***issabon***. That's what a woman will experience. As it turns out, the "toil" of cultivating the earth, which the man will experience, is the same Hebrew word, *issabon*. Woman and man, each responsible for a personal choice, each treated equally by God, each will have a life of *issabon*.

What have you done? Let's look at the ground under our feet...is it littered with apple cores?

"The days of our life are seventy years,

19

or perhaps eighty, if we are strong;
even then their span is only toil and trouble;
they are soon gone, and we fly away." Psalm 90:10

What Was the Original Sin?

"For I am ready to fall, and my pain is ever with me.
I confess my iniquity; I am sorry for my sin." Psalm 38:17-18

We've all heard of "original sin", right? Could you name that
sin? Wasn't it that apple incident in Genesis 3? Would you be
surprised to know neither the word "apple" nor the word "sin"
appears in that narrative?

The first mention of sin in our Bible is Gen. 4:7. The LORD
says to Adam and Eve's firstborn, Cain, *"If you do well, will you not be
accepted? And if you do not do well,* **sin** *is lurking at the door; its desire is for
you, but you must master it."* You all know what happens next…the
firstborn son, Cain, kills his brother, Abel.

Do you have a working definition of sin?
>+Breaking one of the Commandments (i.e. defiance of
>God)? (The first family lived long before these were
>given.)
>+Missing the mark? (A literal definition taken from the
>vocabulary of archery)
>+A basic corrupting influence roaming in the universe?
>(The "devil" made me do it.)
>+Something that separates us from God? (Idolatry is
>replacement of God by anything else.)
>+Anything that is in opposition to God's benevolent
>purposes?

You may be familiar with the idea that while we have only one
word for "snow", the Eskimos have more than one word, because they
distinguish among varying types of snow. Well, the Hebrew language
had at least seven words that are translated as "sin". With varying
definitions such as "iniquity", "trespass", "offense", "wickedness",
"transgression", "crime", "mischief", or "perversion" [*amal, asam, awen,
awon, hatta't, pesa, rasa*], these words usually make it into the Bible as the
one word: "sin". The one found in the Genesis 4:7 passage is **hatta't**,
and that literally means "to miss the mark".

The phrase "original sin" was coined by church father Irenaeus (2nd century) and developed by Augustine (5th century). Their idea, based on writings of Paul, was that original sin is an inherited condition transmitted through procreation. (It was Augustine who devised the terrifying concept that unbaptized infants who die go directly to hell!) But none of that is Biblical! The Jewish tradition does not hold the first humans responsible for the sins of humanity.

We can learn much about sin from the 4th chapter of Genesis, where it does originate. God describes it as a predatory animal. Have you ever felt that? And, by Cain's question (whether sarcastic or ingenuous), we learn the heart of the matter: *"Am I my brother's keeper?"* The fifty chapters of Genesis give us many examples of responses to that question:

+Cain & Abel
+Ishmael & Isaac
+Esau & Jacob
+Joseph & his brothers

When we read these narratives, we recognize themes that plague our world still. We may despair that there is no hope for mankind. But, the book of Genesis does give us the answer to Cain's question. In the last chapter of Genesis, we learn the correct response: Joseph *forgives* his brothers and *cares* for them. YES, I am my brother's keeper. The last word is always FORGIVENESS. Thanks be to God!

"Happy are those whose transgression is forgiven, whose sin is covered.
Then I acknowledged my sin to you, and did not hide my iniquity;
I said, 'I will confess my transgressions to the LORD,' and you forgave the guilt of my sin." Psalm 32:1,5

Torah! Torah! Torah!

"Oh, how I love your law!
It is my meditation all day long". Psalm 119:97

Did you ever have to (or try to) memorize the list of all the books of the Bible? Years later, even those who mastered this, if out of practice, can still manage to recite the first five books: Genesis, Exodus, Leviticus, Numbers, Deuteronomy; did you get them right? The Jewish tradition calls these five books ***Torah***.

Generally, *Torah*, is understood as "Law", but the laws and legal codes are just one portion of the entire *Torah*. Literally, the word means "teaching" or "instruction", and it is a derivative of the Hebrew verb that means "to shoot an arrow".

Although the *Torah* is a compilation of many traditions and sources and is not the work of one author, it is sometimes also called ***torat moshe***, that is "instruction of Moses". Moses was not the author, but his authority is dominant. Apart from the narratives in Genesis, Moses is a main character in the rest of the *Torah*.

You may also hear these books grouped under the term ***Pentateuch***. This is the Greek word for "five scrolls" (*pente* = five + *teuchos* = vessel). Essentially, the five books are only one book. Since the original written format would have been a scroll, the length would have been too long to be anything but cumbersome. Therefore, for the sake of convenience, it was divided into five separate scrolls.

For Jews, the *Torah* is the most holy book, above all the other books of the Hebrew Bible. It is believed that by studying and practicing *Torah* one renews intimacy with God. The *Torah* is the "antidote" to the "evil inclination" of humanity, a pathway toward eternal life.

It is also considered the foundational story for the Jewish people. The fact that stories predominate means that it is a very effective teaching tool. Thanks be to God!

"Hear, my child, your father's instruction [torah],

and do not reject your mother's teaching [torah];
for they are a fair garland for your head,
and pendants for your neck." Proverbs 1:8-9

Toledoth

"Abraham took another wife, whose name was Keturah. She bore him Zimran, Jokshan, Medan, Midian, Ishbak, and Shuah. Jokshan was the father of Sheba and Dedan. The sons of Dedan were Asshurim, Letushim, and Leummim. The sons of Midian were Ephah, Epher, Hanock, Abida, and Eldaah." Genesis 25:1-4

Every lector dreads it. The boring listing of unpronounceable names: Mehujael…Mahalalel…Arpachshad…*really?* These are the Words of Life?

In the book of Genesis alone, we find ten such genealogies. Is this just a literary device to bridge sections? Why are they included? The Hebrew word for these is **toledoth**. The Bible seems regularly punctuated by *toledoth*.*

Most ancient cultures viewed life as cyclical, just like the seasons of the year. The lives of individuals were not of value. If entire populations were wiped out, others would take their place. All that mattered was that there would be farmers or soldiers to serve the king.

But the Hebrew people had a different perspective. *Toledoth* was more than just keeping bloodlines or tribal affiliations orderly. *Toledoth* supported the concept that, being made in the image of God, every individual was *valued* by God. Being remembered by God *was* life.

So when you encounter those boring begats, imagine it is YOUR name.

This is the Word of the Lord…Thanks be to God!

---

*A further note about *toledoth*:

"When Adam had lived one hundred thirty years, he became the father of a son in his likeness, according to his image, and named him Seth. The days of Adam after he became the father of Seth were eight hundred years; and he had other sons and

daughters. Thus all the days that Adam lived were nine hundred thirty years; and he died." Genesis 5:3-4

Frequently the *toledoth* listings included age spans, and many of these are such large numbers that we ask ourselves if people really lived that long. But these ages do not represent longevity, instead they suggest the greatness or goodness of the person: the older, the greater. Other near eastern literature also gives exaggerated ages. An ancient Mesopotamian text listing Sumerian kings reports life spans in the thousands. Realistic age spans are suggested in Psalm 90:10: *"The days of our lives are seventy years, or perhaps eighty, if we are strong."*

God's Memory

In the Bible, the theme of special birth circumstances surfaces so frequently that it has a name, the *"barren woman tradition"*. Women who remain barren for years suddenly give birth to a very special child. From the Old Testament, we could name Samuel's mother, Hannah, who was quite old, but she prayed to God for child and was given one at last. We remember that Samson's mother had been barren for years and years. In the New Testament, Elizabeth, the mother of John the Baptist, was advanced in age, too.

Special births, in the Bible and other traditions, portend the importance or uniqueness of the child born. For example, many believed Julius Caesar was destined to be great because he was born by Caesarean section (hence the term). Of course, Mary of Nazareth, the mother of Jesus, had the most unusual circumstance of all.

In Genesis, the matriarch Sarah had been barren a lifespan; Isaac was born when she was in her nineties. Her situation was so extreme (being beyond menopause) that the prophet Isaiah used her as an example to encourage the Jewish people during their exile to "keep the faith". Later, Isaac's wife, Rebekah, despaired that she remained barren many years. When she finally did become pregnant, she suffered dreadfully as the twins, Esau and Jacob, struggled mightily in the womb. In the next generation after that, Jacob's wife Rachel, too, remained barren for years, while pining with jealousy at the children her own sister Leah continued to birth with Jacob. Ultimately, Rachel gave birth to Joseph, who would grow to be a savior of his people, but her happiness did not last long; she died during the childbirth of her second son.

So, why is the barren woman tradition archetypical in Genesis? It shows the precariousness of our existence and our dependence upon God. Genesis clearly claims that God "remembered" each of these barren women. Every time the future seems about to be extinguished, God "remembers", whether it be a barren woman or a covenant with the people. Our very existence...as a family, as a race, as individuals…has always depended upon God's memory. Thanks be to God.

"She made this vow: 'O LORD of hosts, if only you will look on the misery of your servant, and remember me, and not forget your servant, but will give to your servant a male child, then I will set him before you…'" 1 Samuel 1:11

Angelic Messengers

"I am going to send an angel in front of you, to guard you on the way and to bring you to the place that I have prepared. Be attentive to him and listen to his voice; do not rebel against him, for he will not pardon your transgression; for my name is in him." Exodus 23:20-21

Do you know who was the first person in the Bible to see an angel? If you had to make a guess, would you think it was an Israelite or a non-Israelite? How about a man or a woman? The first recorded visit of an angel to a human in the Bible was to Hagar, the Egyptian servant of Sarah, wife of Abraham, as related in the 16th chapter of Genesis: *"The angel of the LORD found her by a spring of water in the wilderness." (Genesis 16:7)* By the end of their conversation, Hagar speaks as if it was the Lord himself and not just an angel who had visited her.

The patriarch Abraham has an encounter with an angel, as well. In the 22nd chapter of Genesis, it will be an angel who stays Abraham's hand from the near-sacrifice of his beloved son. The Hebrew word that is translated as angel is **mal'ak**. It is literally the word for *"messenger"*, and indeed, many of the times *mal'ak* is encountered in the Old Testament, it is referring to a human messenger.

The same will be true in the New Testament. We get our English word *angel* from the Greek word *angelos*, which is literally *"messenger"*.

Sometimes the Bible stories make it difficult to separate angelic appearances from visitations by the Lord himself. The example of Hagar, above, suggests this was true. There is another story, coming between our two examples so far (Hagar in Genesis 16 and Abraham in Genesis 22), that has mysterious visitors:

"The LORD appeared to Abraham by the oaks of Mamre, as he sat at the entrance of his tent in the heat of the day. He looked up and saw three men standing near him. When he saw them, he ran from the tent entrance to meet them, and bowed down to the ground." (Genesis 18:1-2)

Abraham rushes to prepare a sumptuous feast for the travelers, who then foretell that Abraham and Sarah will have a son in due time. When Sarah laughs aloud at this idea, it is suddenly the Lord himself who is speaking to Abraham there under the oaks at Mamre. In this story, however, the Hebrew word *mal'ak* is never used. The visitors are not even called "men of God" initially—just "three men".

Because the men deliver a message from God, it has become an assumption that they must have been *mal'ak*, to the extent that artwork depicting the scene will show the three with wings. Beyond that, Christians frequently read back into the story their own understanding of who the "three men" must have been: the Trinity, of God the Father, Jesus the Son, along with the Holy Spirit. The text will not support this, of course. The concept of the Trinity developed long after the books that make up our Bible were written. It was early church fathers in the first hundreds of years after Jesus who grappled with this idea of a Trinity and worked out the details we profess in our creeds.

Now for a really grand Bible story about a *mal'ak* you will want to read Numbers 22:20-35, and here is a teaser: *"The donkey saw the angel of the LORD standing in the road, with a drawn sword in his hand, so the donkey turned off the road."* Yes, the Bible has a story about a talking donkey! Thanks be to God!

"...Then Gideon perceived that it was the angel of the LORD; and Gideon said, 'Help me, Lord God! For I have seen the angel of the LORD face to face.' But the Lord said to him, 'Peace be to you; do not fear, you shall not die.' Then Gideon built an altar there to the LORD, and called it, The LORD is peace. To this day it still stands at Ophrah." Judges 6:22-24

Ready, Willing & Able

"Moses was keeping the flock of his father-in-law Jethro, the priest of Midian; he led his flock beyond the wilderness, and came to Horeb, the mountain of God. There the angel of the LORD appeared to him in a flame of fire out of a bush; he looked, and the bush was blazing, yet it was not consumed. Then Moses said, 'I must turn aside and look at this great sight, and see why the bush is not burned up.' When the LORD saw that he had turned aside to see, God called to him out of the bush, 'Moses, Moses!' And he said, 'Here I am.'" Exodus 3:1-4

How often do you tell someone, "Here I am"? Probably often enough that it's not much more than giving your "GPS" (global positioning location!). Maybe your household is busy enough that someone is always calling out, "Where are you?" (Oh, that sounds vaguely familiar…wasn't that God's question in the garden?) The phrase "Here I am" shows up regularly in the Bible, too. You should know that when phrases recur, one should probably dig deeper.

The prophet Isaiah responded to God's call with "Here I am" (Isaiah 6:8). The boy Samuel responded to Eli, when God had called the boy, with "Here I am" (1 Samuel 3:4). Moses responded to God in the burning bush (Exodus 3:4) with "Here I am." Jacob twice responds to God's calling (Genesis 31:1 and 46:2) with "Here I am." Even Mary, in Luke 1:38, responds to the angel's annunciation with "Here I am."

The first Biblical occurrence of the phrase, though, is in the 22nd chapter of Genesis, where it is used so often it sounds like a refrain. It is in the 22nd chapter of Genesis that we read the story of Abraham "binding" Isaac in preparation for sacrificing his beloved son, at the command of God. Abraham responds to God with "Here I am," he responds to Isaac with "Here I am," and he responds to the angel of the Lord with "Here I am." But, this story is much more than a cautionary tale about child sacrifice. It is a true turning point in the Abraham cycle; God will learn that Abraham has absolute, unswerving trust in God. The story is so important in rabbinic theology, that it is incorporated into the daily Jewish liturgy.

So, what's the big deal with the response "Here I am"? First of all, there is no good English equivalent for the Hebrew word, ***hineni.***

31

In Hebrew the phrase captures all the essence of alertness, attentiveness, readiness, receptivity, and responsiveness. The dream response every parent would wish for from a child would be *hineni*, i.e. *"I'm ready, willing, and able...and eager!"* Keep this in mind whenever you encounter "Here I am" in the Bible!

And, be ready with your own response; as the psalmist says in Psalm 40:7-8: *"Here I am...I delight to do your will."* Thanks be to God.

God's in His Heaven

"Turn again, O God of hosts;
look down from heaven and see;
have regard for this vine,
the stock that your right hand planted." Psalm 80:14

Do you believe that God lives in heaven? Perhaps more than any of the Biblical references to God residing in heaven, the famous Robert Browning couplet would be what is recited by many of us in support of this idea:

"God's in his Heaven,
and all's right with the world."

Actually the Bible is rather ambiguous about this place called heaven. In the beginning, according to the Genesis creation story, we learn that God created the heavens and populated the space with celestial entities, sun and moon and stars. Later, characters in Genesis credit God with this creation of heaven:

"And King Melchizedek of Salem brought out bread and wine; he was priest of God Most High. He blessed him and said, "Blessed be Abram by God Most High, maker of heaven and earth." (Genesis 14:18-19)

So, if God created heaven, where did he dwell before then?

In a story in Exodus, God calls Moses and seventy elders of Israel to approach and worship him. When they began to ascend Mt Sinai, the mountain of God (where Moses had had his original meeting with God, according to Exodus 3), one of the first things they notice is God's feet were on a blue pavement:

"They saw the God of Israel. Under his feet there was something like a pavement of sapphire stone, like the very heaven for clearness." (Exodus 24:10)

A vision described by the prophet Ezekiel also suggests that God was above *"something like a throne, in appearance like sapphire"* (Ezekiel 1:26).

An intriguing interpretation is that the sapphire-blue "pavement" upon which God's feet tread is the blue sky we see above. In that case, beyond that blue sky is where God would be found.

As mentioned above, the geography of "heaven" is quite vague in the Bible, but by the Middle Ages, an idea was widespread that God's dwelling place must be a place of pure light, indeed, the source of the light of creation.

This fiery abode beyond the heavenly sky we see was called the **empyrean**. The name is based on a Greek word with the root **pyr**, which is "fire". You may have heard it called "light inaccessible". In Renaissance art, when you see golden areas in the sky, especially with rays of golden light shining forth, it is meant to be the *empyrean*. Sometimes this shows up within a "window" of a cloud opening, and possibly you will see God the Father peaking out or the Holy Spirit dropping down from the golden, fiery *empyrean*.

All sorts of intriguing possibilities stem from this concept. The word *seraphim*, those angelic beings who surrounded the Lord (Isaiah 6:2), means "those who burn". Indeed, some Renaissance art depicting seraphim will have little flames sprouting from their foreheads. Where else in the Bible do we find little flames atop heads? (Check out Acts 2:1-4.)

Along with the idea of the *empyrean*, came the concept of *"created light"* and *"uncreated light"*. Created light includes sunlight, firelight, even electric lights. On the other hand, uncreated light is the very essence of the divine.

This essence is found in the 8th chapter of John's Gospel, in verse 12, Jesus claims, *"I am the light of the world."* Then just two verses later Jesus says, *"I know where I have come from and where I am going."*

This fiery essence shines forth in theophanies throughout the Bible:

+Moses encountered God in the burning bush (Exodus 3:1-6).

+The Israelites in the wilderness were led by God in a pillar of flame (Exodus 40:38) at night.

34

+Elijah experienced this fiery nature in a chariot (2 Kings 2:11-12) that carried him into heaven.

+The three disciples Peter, James, and John witness Jesus, with Moses and Elijah, *transfigured* before their very eyes, and Jesus' *"face shone like the sun"* (Matthew 17:1-8).

So, does God dwell in the *empyrean*? Undoubtedly an attribute of the divine is this fiery nature attested in scripture. But perhaps the dwelling of God is someplace much closer:

+*"Then the cloud covered the tent of meeting, and the glory of the LORD filled the tabernacle." (Exodus 40:35)* God, in the Tabernacle, accompanies the Israelites on their sojourn through the wilderness.

+*"When the priests came out of the holy place, a cloud filled the house of the LORD, so that the priests could not stand to minister because of the cloud; for the glory of the LORD filled the house of the LORD." (1 Kings 8:10-13)* God's very presence fills the Temple which King Solomon had constructed.

+Ezekiel envisions a future Temple surrounded by city precincts for all the people of Israel: *"And the name of the city from that time on shall be, The LORD is There." (Ezekiel 48:35)* Thanks be to God!

And the loveliest passage of all is found at the conclusion of our Bible:

"And I heard a loud voice from the throne saying,
'See, the home of God is among mortals.
He will dwell with them;
they will be his peoples,
and God himself will be with them;
He will wipe every tear from their eyes.
Death will be no more;
mourning and crying and pain will be no more,
for the first things have passed away.'

And the one who was seated on the throne said, 'See I am making all things new.'"
(Revelation 21:3-4)

What's in a Name?

"No longer shall your name be Abram [exalted ancestor]*, but your name shall be Abraham* [ancestor of a multitudes]*." Exodus 17:5*

In the 30th chapter of Genesis, patriarch Jacob has begun fathering sons (origin of the Twelve Tribes of Israel), with his wives in obvious competition. This story of dueling pregnancies is characterized by the names given the baby boys. The chapter is as much about the chosen names as it is about the births. For example, Leah names her last son Zebulun, which is "Honor", because she hoped "my husband now will *honor* me, because I have borne him six sons."

Names reflected the destiny (or the desired destiny!) of the individual. You may have noticed how often the suffix "-el" ends masculine names: Samuel, Michael, Ishmael, Israel, Ezekiel, Joel. El was a word for God, so these names suggest an attribute having to do with God. Ezekiel translates to "May God strengthen this child", while Samuel means "God has heard".

Prophet Hosea is told to name his children according to the behavior of God's people, in an extended metaphor. (Hosea 1:2-9, 2:20-23)

When the King James Version of the Bible was created in the early 1600's, by the order of King James I of England, the various committees doing the translation were given specific guidelines. One of these concerned how the Hebrew names were to be handled. Would they keep the Hebrew words or would they render them in an English form? Obviously, they were instructed to keep the Hebrew words. Otherwise, we'd have a very different-sounding Bible; names like Keziah, Jemimah, and Keren-happuch (the three daughters of Job, Job 42:14) would have been given as Cinnamon, Dove, and Eye-shadow—much more fun for lectors!

Sadly the names of the mothers of Jacob's sons also reflect their "destiny", or at least their relationship with Jacob. While Rachel would translate to "little ewe lamb", Leah would be "wild cow". So, as you read the stories in Genesis…indeed, throughout the Old

Testament…be sure to check out any footnotes to discover the English renditions of the names, whenever they are provided. Thanks be to God.

"My enemies wonder in malice when I will die, and my name perish.
But you, O LORD, be gracious to me, and raise me up, that I may repay them."
Psalm 41:5,10

Whom Do You Serve?

"The Egyptians became ruthless in imposing tasks on the Israelites, and made their lives bitter with hard service in mortar and brick and in every kind of field labor. They were ruthless in all the tasks that they imposed on them." Exodus 1:13-14

The book of Exodus opens with the family of Israelites enslaved under Pharaoh, a Pharaoh who was paranoid at the population growth of the Israelites. In the passage above, we get a hint of their oppression in bondage to Pharaoh.

In the creation story of Genesis, we remember that God had created humankind in his own image. This is a stark contrast to other ancient near eastern creation myths, such as that of the Babylonians. In those other myths, humans had been created to be slaves for the deities. The creation story of Genesis is an intentional contrast; we were not created to be slaves.

The Hebrew word for "to serve" is **abad.** *Abad* means "to work" or "to toil", but it also can mean "to worship"! Egyptian Pharaohs considered themselves deities; the people were expected to give all forms of *abad* to Pharaoh. Let's hear the verses above translated in a fashion that more literally points out all the uses of the word *abad* in the text: *So they made the people SERVE with rigor, and they made their lives bitter with back-breaking SERVICE in mortar and brick, and every kind of SERVICE in the field. With every kind of SERVICE they made them SERVE with rigor.*

This translation in English may not be as polished, with all the repetitions, but that is exactly what we are supposed to be hearing in the passage. God is about to enter a tug-of-war with Pharaoh over whom the people should be serving.

"The Israelites groaned under their slavery, and cried out. Out of the slavery their cry for help rose up to God. God heard their groaning, and God remembered his covenant." Exodus 2:23-24

So, God gets the attention of a shepherd tending his flocks in Midian...Moses.

"Then the LORD said, 'I have observed the misery of my people who are in Egypt; I have heard their cry on account of their taskmasters. Indeed, I know their sufferings, and I have come down to deliver them from the Egyptians, and to bring them up out of that land to a good and broad land...The cry of the Israelites has now come to me; I have also seen how the Egyptians oppress them. So, I will send you to Pharaoh to bring my people...out of Egypt...I will be with you...when you have brought the people out of Egypt, you shall worship God on this mountain.'" Exodus 3:7-12

The first remarkable thing about this paragraph is all the first-person verbs that the Lord God speaks. This tells us our God is present and concerned and active. But the second remarkable thing is what the people will be expected to do: *abad* God! God desires our *abad*, not as slaves, of course, but in the form of priestly and liturgical service. Does that happen in the story? Stay tuned! Thanks be to God!

"Ascribe to the LORD, O families of the peoples,
Ascribe to the LORD glory and strength.
Ascribe to the LORD the glory due his name;
Bring an offering, and come into his courts.
Worship the LORD in holy splendor;
Tremble before him, all the earth." Psalm 96:7-9

I Am Not a Man of Words

"But Moses said to the LORD, 'O my Lord, I have never been eloquent, neither in the past nor even now that you have spoken to your servant; but I am slow of speech and slow of tongue.' Then the LORD said to him, 'Who gives speech to mortals? Who makes them mute or deaf, seeing or blind? Is it not I, the LORD? Now go, and I will be with your mouth and teach you what you are to speak.'" Exodus 4:10-12

A great many of us have experienced "stage fright" at some point in our lives. So, it's easy to identify with Moses in this story of his experience at the burning bush. Do you think his objection was based on fear?

Perhaps he really was a "man of few words", having spent all his adult life in the wilderness of Midian as a shepherd. Or, could it be he recognized that he was not trained in persuasive oratory, so he had a natural aversion to public speaking? Maybe he had a physical speech impediment or impairment of some type. This is never mentioned elsewhere in the Bible, but there is much speculation among scholars. It is even possible he just meant he was no longer fluent in Egyptian, since he had not heard it spoken in decades!

Since this particular objection to God's call was not Moses' only one, could he just be making excuses? Send someone else! Even more of us can surely identify with that trait. At every excuse given, however, God offered Moses the support he would need.

For someone who felt he was not a man of words, it is remarkable that a huge chunk of the Old Testament is devoted to his adventures. Plus, he is credited with delivering the "Ten Words" (***Decalogue*** in Greek) that have been the foundation for legal systems for millennia.

Moses' complaint is echoed by a man responsible for a large chunk of our New Testament—Paul. There are a couple of passages in his second letter to the Corinthians which suggest similar concerns. From 2 Corinthians 10:10: *"...his bodily presence is weak, and his speech contemptible."* And a few verses later (11:6): *"I may be untrained in speech, but not in knowledge."*

41

We all have ready excuses, but God just as readily offers us the support we need, if we go by the main characters in the Bible. Thanks be to God!

"May the words of my mouth and the meditation of my heart be acceptable to you, O LORD, my rock and my redeemer." Psalm 19:14.

Mountaintop Experiences

"Who shall ascend the hill of the LORD?
And who shall stand in his holy place?" Psalm 24:3

It is remarkable how many men in Bible stories encounter God when they've ascended a mountain. We could name Abraham, who had a theophany (an experience of the divine) atop Mt Moriah (Genesis 22), where he had gone to sacrifice his beloved son, at God's command. Jewish tradition is that Mt Moriah is the exact location where the Temple was built centuries later (where God's own beloved Son will reveal himself)!

Moses had his theophanies atop Mt Sinai—both in the burning bush incident (Exodus 3) and where he received the commandments (Exodus 20). Moses' brother Aaron met his death…and God…atop Mt Hor (Numbers 20); Moses himself met God for the last time on Mt Nebo (Deuteronomy 34) at his own death. Upon their entry into the promised land, the people of God were to proclaim the covenant blessings and consequences, with half of them atop Mt Gerizim and the other half atop Mt Ebal (Deuteronomy 27).

Elijah experienced the divine atop Mt Carmel (I Kings 18). Even Jesus climbed mountains to be nearer God—check out Luke 9:28-36 and Luke 22:39. Is the Bible teaching us something about pinnacles, or are they just metaphoric? It is interesting how often the Bible stories place men on mountaintops.

What about women? You may be surprised, but there is also a geographical location that seems to reflect the feminine! In Genesis 16, Hagar, mother to Ishmael, becomes the first character in the Bible to see an angel, who then shows her a well. Isaac's wife, Rebekah, is met at a well. Jacob will meet his wife, Rachel, at a well. In Exodus, Moses meets his wife, Zipporah, at a well. As the source for water, wells are symbolic of life itself. The very longest recorded conversation with Jesus takes place with a woman at a well (John 4).

Considering these parallels is one of the fascinating aspects of Bible study. Thanks be to God!

"I lift up my eyes to the hills—from where will my help come?
My help comes from the LORD, who made heaven and earth." Psalm 121:1-2

Guide Me, O Thou Great Jehovah

"The LORD will guide you continually,
and satisfy your needs in parched places,
and make your bones strong;
and you shall be like a watered garden,
like a spring of water,
whose waters never fail." Isaiah 58:11

So, the focus of this essay is *not* the word *"guide"* (that is a red herring!). No, this is a look at a word that is not found in the Bible. We think it is, probably due to its frequency of use, such as the first line of the great Welsh hymn, "Guide Me, O Thou Great Jehovah". In fact, God's name is not actually Jehovah, and the word is not Biblical. Why, then, is it so commonly used?

When Moses encounters God at the burning bush in Exodus 3:13-15, during their conversation, Moses asks what God's name is. He is told three rather puzzling titles, all of which relate to God's "existence", and none of which is a proper noun such as we might recognize as a name.

Verse 14 gives *"**Ehyeh-Asher-Ehyeh**"* in Hebrew, translated into English by three possibilities: *"I am who I am",* or *"I am what I am"* or *"I will be who I will be".* Next, verse 14 gives *"**Ehyeh**",* or just *"I am".* Finally verse 15, offers *"**YHWH**",* which will not actually be printed in the Bible. Jews avoided speaking this holy name, and to avoid speaking it, they avoided writing it. As a substitution, they wrote the Hebrew word for *the Lord,* which is **Adonai.** In English translations of the Bible, this will be shown as "the LORD", with all caps. Check throughout this book, as well; all the opening quotations which have the name of God spell it "LORD", in all capital letters.

That still does not reveal how the word *"Jehovah"* came to be used. First, we must realize that initially Hebrew words printed in the Bible did not include any vowels. These were later added. Since YHWH is not pronounced, it was just assumed that the missing vowels between the consonants should be the same vowel sounds as heard in the word *Adonai.* Then, we must remember that before there were English translations of the Hebrew Bible, Latin translations were made.

Since the Latin language does not have either a letter "Y" or a letter "W", substitutions had to be made for those letters, which resulted in "JHVH. Now it is readily seen that when we add the vowel sounds of *Adonai* into the **tetragrammaton** (fancy Greek word for "four letters"!), the result is *Jehovah*.

There are actually many different words and titles applied to God throughout the Bible. All are feeble attempts to use our own language and understanding to describe the Creator of the Universe. But I suspect God will hear us whichever title we do use. Thanks be to God!

"God also said to Moses, 'Thus you shall say to the Israelites, 'The LORD, the God of your ancestors, the God of Abraham, the God of Isaac, and the God of Jacob, has sent me to you:
This is my name forever,
And this is my title for all generations.'" Exodus 3:15

Hardened Heart

"And the LORD said to Moses, 'When you go back to Egypt, see that you perform before Pharaoh all the wonders that I have put in your power; but I will harden his heart, so that he will not let the people go.'" Exodus 4:21

"So the heart of Pharaoh was hardened, and he would not let the Israelites go, just as the LORD had spoken through Moses." Exodus 9:35

When one reads the beginning of the Exodus story, it is usually troubling to think that God is the one that causes Pharaoh's heart to be hardened, thereby lengthening all the drama of the plagues. Wouldn't it have been easier to *soften* his heart? Indeed, after each of the plagues, we read that either Pharaoh hardened his heart or God hardened his heart. [Check out Exodus 7:13; 7:22; 8:15; 8:19; 8:32; 9:7; 9:12; 9:34.] Was Pharaoh predestined to be the villain?

Granted, Pharaoh is stubborn and does not recognize the God of the Israelites. God, however, does not cause or initiate Pharaoh's stubbornness; it is not predestination! It is, in fact, more of a response to Pharaoh's own initiation and continuation of hard-heartedness.

The Hebrew word for the hardening is **kabed.** It means to "weigh heavy", as in "to have importance", but it can also be translated as "to have honor". It has the sense of "abounding" in either a bad or a good way. The intention of the passages about Pharaoh is that God allows Pharaoh the full expression of his hardening heart. Pharaoh abounds in his stubbornness.

In the latter half of the book of Exodus, after Egypt has been vanquished and God is leading the people out of bondage (of body, mind, and spirit), we will see the same word, *kabed*, describing the glory ascribed to God! [See Exodus 16:7; 16:10; 24:16-17; 29:43; 33:18; 33:22; 40:34-35.] The full expression of the glory of God will abound.

The same word applied to both Pharaoh in the early chapters and then to God in the later chapters emphasizes the tug-of-war for the people's allegiance, for either their service [remember that word, *abad*] as slaves or their worship [the same word, *abad*] of God as the people of God. Exodus concludes with the latter. Thanks be to God!

47

"Then the cloud covered the tent of meeting, and the glory [kabed] of the LORD filled the tabernacle. Moses was not able to enter the tent of meeting because the cloud settled upon it, and the glory [kabed] of the LORD filled the tabernacle." Exodus 40:34-35

God Remembered

"God heard their groaning, and God remembered his covenant with Abraham, Isaac, and Jacob. God looked upon the Israelites, and God took notice of them." Exodus 2:24-25

"God also spoke to Moses and said to him: 'I am the LORD. ...I have also heard the groaning of the Israelites whom the Egyptians are holding as slaves, and I have remembered my covenant.'" Exodus 6:2,5

We all forget things. You know how easily things we are supposed to remember just "slip from our minds".

Upon first blush, the idea that God remembered his covenant sounds reassuring, right? Upon second thought, however, we may wonder if that means God had forgotten it up until then. Have you wondered about that?

A vocabulary lesson will set us straight about the verb "remember", as used in the Old Testament. In English, of course, we place the verb "remember" against its antonym, "forget". For us, both verbs describe thought processes. When we remember something, we call forth or contemplate a bit of information; when we forget something, thoughts about it just do not show up at all.

The Hebrew word translated as "remember" is **zakhor.** *Zakhor* is more than a thought process of recall or recognition. In Hebrew there is intentional action that follows an act of *zakhor.* Sometimes it will be translated into English as "mention" and not as "remember" in the Old Testament.

Zakhor is recalling something or someone from the past and then actively focusing on that in the present. It does not suggest that the object was ever forgotten; it was just not acted upon...yet. As used in the Old Testament, when God remembers, we do not have to worry that God has ever forgotten. No, God remembering anything means God is about to take action. In the Hebrew narratives of God, *zakhor* lets us know God is about to act on behalf of others. Thanks be to God!

"God said, 'This is the sign of the covenant that I make between me and you and every living creature that is with you, for all future generations: I have set my bow in the clouds, and it shall be a sign of the covenant between me and the earth. When I bring clouds over the earth and the bow is seen in the clouds, I will remember my covenant that is between me and you and every living creature of all flesh; and the waters shall never again become a flood to destroy all flesh. When the bow is in the clouds, I will see it and remember the everlasting covenant between God and every living creature of all flesh that is on the earth.'" *Genesis 9:12-16*

Forty Days

"For in seven days I will send rain on the earth for forty days and forty nights; and every living thing that I have made I will blot out from the face of the ground."
Genesis 7:4

"Moses was there with the LORD forty days and forty nights; he neither ate bread nor drank water. And he wrote on the tablets the words of the covenant, the ten commandments." Exodus 34:28

Have you ever noticed how frequently a time-span of forty days is part of the stories in the Bible? Not only do we have the examples above, about Noah and the flood and then Moses receiving the commandments, but can you think of some other examples?

Actually it happened twice to Moses; the first time is in Exodus 24:18. Elijah was fasting on Mt. Horeb (1 Kings 19:8) forty days and forty nights. That's how long the spies Moses sent were in Canaan (Numbers 13:25). That's how long Jonah told Nineveh it had left before it would be overturned (Jonah 3:4). The first three Gospel accounts in the New Testament record that Jesus fasted in the wilderness for forty days (Matthew 4:2; Mark 1:13; Luke 4:2).

And even longer than forty days would be the forty years that the Israelites spent wandering in the wilderness in the Exodus story. Is forty just supposed to be a convenient number to choose for anything that lasts a long period of time? There is number symbolism throughout the Bible. Four is usually associated with earthly or created things, i.e. four seasons; four winds; four cardinal directions; four phases of the moon each month; and the ancients thought everything was composed of the four elements of earth, water, air, and fire. During the Medieval era, it was thought that four angels were at the four corners of the world, holding the four winds.

Ten is a number that is associated with human completeness, i.e. ten fingers, ten toes, the decimal system, the metric system, the ten commandments, etc. So, multiplying the earthly number, 4, by the human number, 10, we get 40, which can be used to stand for a dimension of human suffering.

Although this seems to be true, there is more to it. In all of these Bible stories, the forty days (or years) are frequently described as a time of testing, but it is important to keep reading. In each instance, the span of time is necessary as a period for preparation. Noah must prepare to be the new beginning for humanity. Moses must prepare for presenting God's covenant to the Israelites. Jesus must prepare for his ministry and his mission. It is no accident that the early church designated the season of Lent to be forty days (not counting Sundays!). It was used as a preparation time for those who would be baptized at Easter. It is used by many as a time of penitence to prepare for the celebration of Easter. If you observe Lent, consider how you will use it as preparation. For what purpose might you prepare? Thanks be to God!

"So perish all your enemies, O LORD!
But may your friends be like the sun as it rises in the night.
And the land had rest forty years." Judges 5:31

Sibling Rivalry

"Isaac prayed to the LORD for his wife, because she was barren; and the LORD granted his prayer, and his wife Rebekah conceived. The children struggled together within her; and she said, 'If it is to be this way, why do I live?' So she went to inquire of the LORD. And the LORD said to her, 'Two nations are in your womb, and two peoples born of you shall be divided; the one shall be stronger than the other, the elder shall serve the younger.'" Genesis 25:21-23

Daytime soap-operas on television have nothing on the dysfunctional families in Genesis. Readers of Genesis cannot help but notice a pervasive pattern of sibling rivalry, sometimes beginning before birth, as in the passage quoted above. But case studies could also be written from the tales of blended families, step children, surrogacy, deception, polygamy, fratricide, irksome in-laws, mass murderers, and more in this first book of our Bible. And that's just among the men-folk. The story of daughter Dinah in chapter 34 or that of daughter-in-law Tamar in chapter 38 are both R-rated and never make it into the Sunday lectionary of readings!

At the time of the patriarchs, special privileges attached to the firstborn son of a family: a birthright and a larger portion of inheritance. That tradition gets derailed amongst the patriarchs in every single generation of the family! First, patriarch Abraham's eldest son, Ishmael, is banished by step-mom Sarah, leaving the full inheritance to the younger Isaac. This same Isaac will be duped by his wife and the younger of his twin sons into giving the special blessing to younger Jacob instead of to elder Esau.

The favoritism and jealousies are perpetuated within Jacob's family circle, with the ten older brothers hating the favored younger, Joseph. They end up selling him into slavery; when father Jacob thinks Joseph is dead, he transfers the favoritism to youngest brother, Benjamin.

With these reversals occurring every generation, of the elder being supplanted somehow by the younger, we are not surprised when Judah's twin sons get "reversed" at the moment of their birth (Genesis 38:27-29) or when Joseph's sons accidentally get reversed blessings, the younger over the elder (Genesis 48:17-20).

These very human stories certainly give us ample opportunity to find our own story somewhere in the mix. With whom do you identify?

Why is the special status of the first-born repeatedly turned upside down in Genesis? Maybe that's the problem; awarding special status to any one above another is a purely human convention. No matter who deserves or receives the most of anything is not as important as who is open to hearing the voice of God and seeking his will. The only selection process that matters is with whom God can work. Thanks be to God!

"Then Joseph could no longer control himself before all those who stood by him, and he cried out, 'Send everyone away from me.' So no one stayed with him when Joseph made himself known to his brothers. And he wept so loudly that the Egyptians heard it, and the household of Pharaoh heard it. …Then Joseph said to his brothers, 'Come closer to me.' And they came closer. He said, 'I am your brother, Joseph, whom you sold into Egypt. And now do not be distressed, or angry with yourselves, because you sold me here; for God sent me before you to preserve life.'"
Genesis 45:1-2,4-5

First-Fruits, Firstlings, Firstborn

"On the day of the first fruits, when you offer a grain offering of new grain to the LORD at your festival of weeks, you shall have a holy convocation; you shall not work at your occupations." Numbers 28:26

Throughout the Old Testament there seems to be a theme of offering the first-fruits of farmers, the firstlings (of animals) from shepherds, and even firstborn sons from new mothers to God. The Hebrew word **b-kor** underlies this "firstness". As stated, the *b-kor* can be applied to grains, as in the verse above and to animals: *"A firstling of animals, however, which as a firstling belongs to the LORD, cannot be consecrated by anyone; whether ox or sheep." (Leviticus 27:26)* These would be sacrificial offerings to God. Firstborn sons would not, of course, be sacrificed, but they were "dedicated" to service of the Lord. A prime example of this is Hannah bringing her son Samuel to the house of the Lord, with thanksgiving: *"For this child I prayed; and the LORD has granted me the petition that I made to him. Therefore I have lent him to the LORD; as long as he lives, he is given to the LORD." She left him there for the LORD. (1 Samuel 1:27-28)*

God also viewed the Israelite people as a *b-kor* to himself: *"Israel was holy to the LORD, the first fruits of his harvest. All who ate of it were held guilty; disaster came upon them, says the LORD." (Jeremiah 2:3)* This is a prominent theme in the book of Exodus. *"Then you shall say to Pharaoh, 'Thus says the LORD: Israel is my firstborn son. I said to you, 'Let my son go that he may worship me." But you refused to let him go; now I will kill your firstborn son.'" (Exodus 4:22-23)*

You know what happens…all the firstborn in Egypt, not protected by the Passover blood as were the Israelite tribes, were struck down: *"For I will pass through the land of Egypt that night, and I will strike down every firstborn in the land of Egypt, both human beings and animals; on all the gods of Egypt I will execute judgments: I am the LORD. The blood shall be a sign for you on the houses where you live; when I see the blood, I will pass over you, and no plague shall destroy you when I strike the land of Egypt." (Exodus 12:12-13)*

Any ideas why the first-fruits, the firstlings, and the firstborn were considered to be God's? It is certainly contrary to the examples among the patriarchs of the younger sons being the chosen ones, whilst all the firstborn sons of the patriarchs were skipped when it came time to pass on the family blessing and inheritance (see essay, *"Sibling Rivalry"*).

Let us go back to the very opening chapters of the Bible, just before the first firstborn son, Cain, murders his younger brother, Abel: *"In the course of time Cain brought to the LORD an offering of the fruit of the ground, and Abel for his part brought of the firstlings of his flock, their fat portions. And the LORD had regard for Abel and his offering, but for Cain and his offering he had no regard. So Cain was very angry, and his countenance fell."* *(Genesis 4:3-5)* People do puzzle over God's preference, so we must take our clues from the only words given in the text. What was Cain's offering? Fruit of the ground, which we are not even told was anything Cain had worked to produce; maybe he had just picked up fruit that had fallen to the ground. The text does tell us that Abel had cared for a flock and then offered to God the very first kids that were born. That shows thankfulness in return for gifts that had been given to him in the first place. Abel's offering perhaps was an acknowledgement of that.

Hmm…an acknowledgement of a gift… *"When Pharaoh stubbornly refused to let us go, the LORD killed all the firstborn in the land of Egypt, from the human firstborn to the firstborn of animals. Therefore I sacrifice to the LORD every male that first opens the womb, but every firstborn of my sons I redeem."* *(Exodus 13:15)* Initially, sacrifices of the firstborn may have been believed, at least culturally, to assure fertility. For the Israelites, tho', especially since their liberation from bondage, things have changed. Just as God took all the firstborn of Egypt, so the firstborn of all Israel belongs to God. But rather than sacrificial death, God desires redemption. Consecration honors that redemption and…acknowledges a gift…of life. Considering all of these passages, our questions may abound about what the text is trying to impart. But the more important question becomes: What are we going to do about it? What are your firstlings? Thanks be to God.

"You are children of the LORD your God…For you are a people holy to the LORD your God; it is you the LORD has chosen out of all the peoples on earth to be his people…" Deuteronomy 14:1-2.

Covenantal Love

"In your steadfast love you led the people whom you redeemed;
you guided them by your strength to your holy abode." Exodus 15:13

Translating some original words from the Bible into English can be rather difficult, because sometimes precise equivalents just do not exist. One word in particular that has caused concern is the Hebrew word ***hesed***. In our verse above, it was translated as "steadfast love". As this phrase, you will encounter it multiple times in the Old Testament, especially in the Psalms. The fullest meaning of the word, however, just cannot be conveyed in English. Various English versions of the Bible have rendered it as "mercy", "loyalty", "goodness", "favor" and "loving-kindness", which is a popular choice that was coined by Bible translator Miles Coverdale in 1535.

Hesed is not "kindness" in general, and it is not used to describe kindness of any type between humans. It is always used to describe God, with the intention of putting forth God's steadfastness and persistence in his love for his covenant-people. *Hesed* is the loving-kindness of God that will not let Israel go, despite Israel's continual waywardness. For this reason it is associated with God's covenant.

We know that God's determination toward the covenant results in God's need to exercise mercy again and again. For this reason, when the Old Testament was translated into Greek in the third century BC, the word *eleos* (mercy, pity) was chosen, and the Latin translation done by Jerome in the fourth century AD used the word *misericordia* (merciful) for *hesed*. The English choice of "steadfast love" comes somewhat closer to the fuller meaning, which is ideally a composite of love with strength and fidelity.

Actually, the English word that is closest to this *hesed* that God gives is "grace". We think of grace as a New Testament word, since that is where we will read it (Greek: *charis*). Martin Luther realized that *hesed* is the equal of *charis*, and he translated both into the German *gnade*, that is *grace* in English.

God's steadfast love, *hesed*, is not a sentimental love, it is a love that abounds in all of the concepts listed above to a degree that is beyond our comprehension or ability to explain. It is undeserved on our part, and forever sure on God's. Thanks be to God!

"The LORD, the LORD,
a God merciful and gracious,
slow to anger,
and abounding in steadfast love
and faithfulness,
keeping steadfast love for the thousandth generation,
forgiving iniquity and
transgression and sin…" Exodus 34:6-7

"Be mindful of your mercy, O LORD,
and of your steadfast love,
for they have been from of old.
Do not remember the sins of my
youth or my transgressions;
according to your steadfast love
remember me, for your goodness' sake, O LORD!" Psalm 25:6-7

Jealous God

"You shall not bow down to them or worship them; for I the LORD your God am a jealous God..." Exodus 20:5

"...for you shall worship no other god, because the LORD, whose name is Jealous, is a jealous God." Exodus 34:14

"For the LORD your God is a devouring fire, a jealous God." Deuteronomy 4:24

The green-eyed monster! Envy...jealousy...traits we do not find to be complimentary. One is even a deadly sin, according to the Roman Catholic tradition that goes back to Pope Gregory in 590 AD. English dictionaries define both words in similar terms. Technically, envy and jealousy are two different emotions. Jealousy is a feeling of discontent toward another for what he has or is, whereas envy is an insatiable desire to deprive another of what is his.

Is it okay to ascribe such a negative emotion to God? Would you be surprised to learn that the Old Testament *only* applies this adjective to God and never to a human!

The Hebrew word that is translated into "jealous" is **qana**. Literally, the word means a strong emotion...for good or bad. An alternative translation is *zealous*. And, indeed, there are times in the Old Testament when *qana* gets translated as *zealous*.

So, what is underlying the use of *qana* as an adjective of God? As a strong emotion, when applied to God, the emotion is one of intense love, a love that is eager to protect what is precious to God. When God is called *qana*, his love is as a husband for a wife, a strong love that expects faithfulness, a love that is *zealous* to protect the relationship.

The third quotation above, from the 4th chapter of Deuteronomy, is followed in Deuteronomy's 5th chapter with a listing of the "ten commandments", which are familiar to most of us. And then in 6th chapter of Deuteronomy, we come to the greatest commandment the Lord gave to his people. The Jewish people call it the "**Shema**". The *Shema* is the central prayer, the prayer that Jewish children learn first. It is the text that will be written out on parchment, rolled up, and placed in a **mezuzah**, that little container attached to the doorpost of a Jewish structure.

The *Shema*, in Judaism, is the response to the *qana* of God, the "human" *qana* right back to God! *"Hear, O Israel: The LORD is our God, the LORD alone. You shall love the LORD your God with all your heart, and with all our soul, and with all your might. Keep these words that I am commanding you today in your heart. Recite them to your children and talk about them when you are at home and when you are away, when you lie down and when you rise. Bind them as a sign on your hand, fix them as an emblem on your forehead, and write them on the doorposts of your house and on your gates."* (Deuteronomy 6:4-9)

If *qana* is the Lord's declaration of love for his bride, then the *Shema* is the wedding vow of the bride for her husband. Thank God for this intense love!

"The zeal of the LORD of hosts will do this." 1 Kings 19:31

Thirteen Attributes of Mercy

"Then Moses turned and went down from the mountain, carrying the two tablets of the covenant in his hands... The tablets were the work of God, and the writing was the writing of God, engraved upon the tablets. ...As soon as he came near the camp, and saw the calf and the dancing, Moses' anger burned hot, and he threw the tablets from his hands and broke them at the foot of the mountain." Exodus 32:15-19

Surely you have heard (or said yourself) that if God were more obvious, then no one would have doubts. If God (or Jesus) would just show up, then we all could readily believe, right? The passage quoted above occurs after Moses had been atop Mt Sinai with God for forty days. What is unbelievable is that just forty days earlier, before Moses went up Sinai, everyone assembled (thousands, according to the account in Exodus) witnessed first-hand the very presence of God. It was a theophany of outrageous magnitude. Yet after forty days (the same number of days that are in the season of Lent), every one of them forgot it all, and melted the golden jewelry taken from Egypt, and formed it into a golden calf to worship. You can read the whole sordid story in the 32nd chapter of Exodus.

Here is something even more amazing. With just one chapter between the incident with the golden calf and the following passage, God speaks these words to Moses:
"The LORD, the LORD,
a God merciful and gracious, slow to anger,
and abounding in steadfast love and faithfulness,
keeping steadfast love for the thousandth generation,
forgiving iniquity and transgression and sin..." (Exodus 34:6-7)

All is forgiven! These verses are the core of an important Jewish prayer, called the **Selichot**, that are recited for forgiveness on days of fasting, on penitential occasions, and during the Days of Awe. The Days of Awe are the ten days of repentance from Rosh Hashanah to Yom Kippur. The *Selichot* is not recited on the Sabbath, because they are for personal petitioning. The Jewish tradition is that if these thirteen attributes of God are recited, in the proper order, then God's mercy is assured.

61

Now you have probably gone back through the verses and tried to count out thirteen specific attributes; I certainly tried to find thirteen and could not. Actually opinions do differ as to the counting. I commend you to "Google", if you desire to see a listing!

We may not have a "sighting" as obvious as the Sinai experience, but every time you open your Bible, prepare for a theophany! Thanks be to God!

"Make me know your ways, O LORD;
teach me your paths.
Lead me in your truth,
and teach me,
For you are the God
of my salvation;
for you I wait all day long.
Be mindful of your mercy, O LORD,
and of your steadfast love,
for they have been from of old.
Do not remember the sins
of my youth or my transgressions;
according to your steadfast love
remember me,
for your goodness' sake, O LORD!" Psalm 25:4-7

The Crimson Cord

Rahab of Jericho let the two Israelite spies "down by a rope through the window, for her house was on the outer side of the city wall and she resided within the wall itself. She said to them, 'Go toward the hill country, so that the pursuers may not come upon you. Hide yourselves there three days, until the pursuers have returned; then afterward you may go your way.' The men said to her, 'We will be released from this oath that you have made us swear to you if we invade the land and you do not tie this crimson cord in the window through which you let us down, and you do not gather into your house your father and mother, your brothers, and all your family.' …She said, 'According to your words, so be it.' She sent them away and they departed. Then she tied the crimson cord in the window." Joshua 2:15-21

Do you remember this Bible story? The Israelites are about to cross the Jordan River into the promised land, and Joshua has sent spies ahead to check out the lay of the enemy land. A woman of the city, Rahab, hides the spies, and in return they promise that she and her family will be spared when the city is taken by the Israelites. The *crimson cord* is how her household is identified and rescued before the walls "come tumblin' down"!

One earlier time there is a story that uses a *crimson cord* to mark something important. In Genesis 38:27-30, the woman Tamar gives birth to twin sons of Judah, son of patriarch Jacob. When the first baby put out his hand, while Tamar was in labor, the midwife tied a crimson cord around the baby's wrist to signify that he was the firstborn son. But then the baby drew his hand back in, and as it happened, the other son, without the crimson cord, was born first. The actual firstborn son, Perez, was to become the ancestor of King David.

These two themes of the *crimson cord* (the first-born and the mark of protection) are mysteriously intertwined with the Passover (**Pesach**) story in the 12th chapter of Exodus. God has told Moses, *"Toward midnight I will go forth among the Egyptians, and every first-born in the land of Egypt shall die, from the first-born of Pharaoh who sits on his throne to the first-born of the female slaves who sit behind the handmill, and all the first-born of the livestock." (Exodus 11:4-5)* God also tells Moses that every family is to take a lamb to slaughter, then to *"take some of the blood and put it on the* *two doorposts and the lintel of the houses in which they are to eat it." (Exodus 12:7)*

The people are told to eat the lamb hurriedly, leaving no leftovers, because *"it is a **pesach** offering to the LORD. (Exodus 12:11)* God said, *"For that night I will go through the land of Egypt and strike down every first-born in the land of Egypt, both man and beast; on all the gods of Egypt I will execute judgment; I am the LORD. The blood shall be a sign for you on the houses where you live; when I see the blood, I will **pesach** you, and no plague shall destroy you when I strike the land of Egypt ." (Exodus 12: 12-13)* Pesach is a glorious word-play in Hebrew. It can mean *passover* (as in leap over), and it can mean *protection*.

Just as Rahab's household was spared from the destruction of Jericho by the sign of a red cord from her window, so all the Israelites were spared from the death of the all first-born humans and animals in Egypt, by the sign of a red slash of blood on the doorposts!

God's further instructions: *"This day shall be a day of remembrance for you. You shall celebrate it as a festival to the LORD; throughout your generations you shall observe it as a perpetual ordinance." (Exodus 12:14)* And, of course, we know that Passover continues to be the primary Jewish high holy observance, even marking the start of their liturgical year. Thanks be to God!

*"So the LORD of hosts will come down
to fight upon Mount Zion and upon its hill.
Like birds hovering overhead; so the LORD of hosts
will **pesach** Jerusalem; he will **pesach** and deliver it,
he will spare and rescue it." (Isaiah 31:4-5)*

Bread from Heaven

"The whole congregation of the Israelites complained against Moses and Aaron in the wilderness. The Israelites said to them, 'If only we had died by the hand of the LORD in the land of Egypt, when we sat by the fleshpots and ate our fill of bread; for you have brought us out into this wilderness to kill this whole assembly with hunger.' Then the LORD said to Moses, 'I am going to rain bread from heaven for you, and each day the people shall go out and gather enough for that day.' ...in the morning there was a layer of dew around the camp. When the layer of dew lifted, there on the surface of the wilderness was a fine flaky substance, as fine as frost on the ground. When the Israelites saw it, they said to one another, 'What is it?' For they did not know what it was. Moses said to them, 'It is the bread that the LORD has given you to eat.'" Exodus 16:2-4, 11-15

In this 16th chapter of Exodus and later in the 11th chapter of Numbers, we learn quite a bit about this strange "bread from heaven". It was on the ground when the dew lifted in the mornings, it was as flaky as frost, it would melt in the sun, and it did not keep until a second day...except on the eve of the Sabbath, when it would last an extra 24 hours, since none would appear on the Sabbath! It was versatile to prepare; it could be baked or boiled. It tasted pleasingly like honeyed wafers. It sustained the people for forty years. Can you imagine eating the same thing every day for forty years?

But here's the thing about **manna** (which, by the way, is the Hebrew for "what is it?"). Everyone got the same amount. There was no surplus; there was no lack. There was no greed. There was no hoarding. There was no hunger. There were no "have's" and "have not's". There were no class distinctions. Quite the economy!

Also, quite the teacher! From this daily miracle of "bread from heaven", the people had to learn to depend on God alone. They had to learn that every moment of their very existence depended upon God alone...and his daily miracles.

Turns out, even today there is a cash product produced in the Sinai called tamarisk manna, made from the crystallized globules that tamarisk plant lice secrete each day. It tastes like honey, abounds in carbohydrates, and is used by the Bedouin as a sweetener. That's the problem with miracles; they are in the eye of the beholder.

You may be surprised to learn that the very familiar Lord's Prayer has a petition requesting manna. Yes, when we pray, *"Give us this day our daily bread,"* we are not being redundant (saying "day" *and* "daily"); the adjective "daily" has in other sources been translated as "supernatural". What bread was "supernatural"? "Bread from heaven"! Thanks be to God!

"Our ancestors ate the manna in the wilderness; as it is written, 'He gave them bread from heaven to eat.' Then Jesus said to them, 'Very truly, I tell you, it was not Moses who gave you the bread from heaven, but it is my Father who gives you the true bread from heaven. For the bread of God is that which comes down from heaven and gives life to the world.' They said to him, 'Sir, give us this bread always.' Jesus said to them, "I am the bread of life."' John 6:31-35

Big Ten

"Then the LORD said, "I do forgive, just as you have asked; nevertheless—as I live , and as all the earth shall be filled with the glory of the LORD—none of the people who have seen my glory and the signs that I did in Egypt and in the wilderness, and yet have tested me these ten times and have not obeyed my voice, shall see the land that I swore to give to their ancestors..." Numbers 14:20-23

Often readers of Bible stories notice how regularly particular numbers pop up in story after story. In a previous essay in this series, we looked at the recurrence and symbolism of the number 40. It was noted that 10 is a number that refers to a dimension of human completeness—ten fingers, ten toes, ten as the base for the decimal place value system and the metric system of measure. There are even nursery rhymes to teach counting to ten: "One little, two little, three little..."; you are probably already singing the tune in your head and completing the verse... "ten little Indian boys." Ten also recurs in Jesus' parables about humanity: ten lepers, ten bridesmaids, ten talents/coins.

Do any Old Testament stories use the number 10? Do you think there were ten plagues that God brought down on Pharaoh? That's how many we remember, right? It is true; ten awesome acts of God are described in the chapters seven through twelve of Exodus. Counting them on your fingers helps you remember them!

If you read any commentaries on Exodus, however, you would learn that it is a documented fact that the Old Testament stories are woven from several strands of ancient texts. You can research this yourself, and you will find that these primary sources are called **J** (*Jehovist*), **E** (*Elohist*), **P** (*Priestly*), and **D** (*Deuteronomist*). At some point these were intertwined into the book we have today. By comparing language use and the themes, it has been determined that each only tells of a much smaller number of plagues. The J-source reports eight plagues, the E-source has five plagues, and the P-source offers five plagues (but differing from the E-source!). All sources concur on the first and the last. Some commentaries might even disagree that the last plague—the death of the firstborn—is to be counted, since it was not "reversed" as the others were; it was the ultimate defeat of Egypt.

And, how about the commandments? Everyone knows there were ten of those, right? True, again…but what are the ten? Counting on your fingers may help you remember them, but would you be surprised to learn that different religious denominations identify different commandments as they count? We find the Bible lists in either Exodus 20 or Deuteronomy 5. One of the differences arises in figuring out which parts of Exodus 20:6-10 count as separate commands. That means that some denominations have the command about not making an idol (graven image) separate from having no other gods, but not all do. Another sticking point is whether Exodus 20:21, regarding coveting, contains one or two commands. So, Catholics and some Protestant groups, and Lutherans and Jews will name different commandments as "the ten"! Does it matter? Not at all! Thanks be to God!

"The LORD said to Moses: Write these words; in accordance with the words I have made a covenant with you and with Israel. He was there with the LORD forty days and forty nights, he neither ate bread nor drank water. And he wrote on the tablets the words of the covenant, the ten commandments." Exodus 34:27-28

Tabernacling with God

"And have them make me a sanctuary so that I may dwell among them." Exodus 25:8

"Moses did everything just as the LORD had commanded him. In the first month in the second year, on the first day of the month, the tabernacle was set up. ...Then the cloud covered the tent of meeting, and the glory of the LORD filled the tabernacle." Exodus 40:16-17, 34

Chapters 25 through 30 in Exodus give us the very detailed description by God for the *tabernacle* that Moses is to lead the Israelite people to construct. Then, chapters 35 through 40 of Exodus tell the story of the people following these instructions just as specified, as the Lord had commanded. When the tabernacle is completed, God moves in!

The tabernacle was a portable, tent-like structure that had varying zones of holiness, with the innermost "Holy of Holies" designated as the place wherein the stone tablets of the covenant (what we would call the "Ten Commandments") were housed within a furnishing called the "Ark of the Covenant".

The tabernacle would accompany the Israelites for their forty years in the wilderness. Whenever they needed to move the camp, the Levite tribe would be in charge of disassembling then later reassembling the tabernacle. Much later, when the people are inhabiting the land of promise, when King Solomon builds the Temple in Jerusalem, the tabernacle will be folded up and stored in the Temple, no longer needed.

In Hebrew, the word that we translate as tabernacle is **mishkan.** In English, *mishkan* is literally an abode, a word that comes from the root **sh-k-n**, which translates as "abide". And related to both of these is the Hebrew word **Shekhinah.** The feminine noun *Shekhinah* is most closely translated as "The Very Presence of God"! So, of course, the whole concept of the tabernacle is that it will be a dwelling place for God, so God can always abide with the people.

The concept transfers into Greek and makes its way into the New Testament, too. In Greek, **eskenosen**, is the verb for "tabernacled". It is to be found in the Prologue of John's Gospel: *"And the Word became flesh and **lived** [tabernacled] among us, and we have seen his glory, the glory as of a father's only son, full of grace and truth." (John 1:14)*

How awesome! The Very Presence of God has pitched his tent to hang out with us! Thanks be to God!

"O LORD, I love the house in which you dwell,
and the place where your glory abides." Psalm 26:8

Mercy Seat

"Then you shall make a mercy seat of pure gold; two cubits and a half shall be its length, and a cubit and a half its width. You shall make two cherubim of gold; you shall make them of hammered work, at the two ends of the mercy seat. Make one cherub at the one end, and one cherub at the other; of one piece with the mercy seat you shall make the cherubim at its two ends. The cherubim shall spread out their wings above, overshadowing the mercy seat with their wings. They shall face one to another; the faces of the cherubim shall be turned toward the mercy seat. You shall put the mercy seat on the top of the ark; and in the ark you shall put the covenant that I shall give you. There I will meet with you, and from above the mercy seat, from between the two cherubim that are on the ark of the covenant, I will deliver to you all my commands for the Israelites." Exodus 25:17-22

The instructions are so specific; can you picture in your mind's eye what this looked like? (A cubit was the length of a man's arm from elbow to finger-tip, about eighteen inches.) Pure gold! Are you able to envision the gleaming shine? As for **cherubim**, do not imagine that these are the smiling, naked baby angels that float in billowy clouds in Renaissance art or the fat faces of angelic babes with wings that predominate in holiday greeting cards. No, *cherubim* (singular, *cherub*) were protective creatures, first encountered in Genesis 3:24. God stationed *cherubim* as guards to the garden of Eden after the humans were expelled. They guarded the entrance with "a fiery, ever-turning sword"!

Now we must conjure up the *mercy seat* in our imaginations. First, you should know that the Hebrew Bible just calls it a *"cover"*! In Hebrew, this cover is **kapporeth**, a word from the verb "to cover", **kaphar**. Of interest is the fact that *kaphar* quite literally means "to wipe out", as in "wipe clean of impurities".

Once a year, on the high holy day of **Yom Kippur** the Jewish high priest would enter the Holy of Holies (the innermost sanctum of the Tabernacle or Temple) and splash sacrificial blood on the *kapporeth*, praying this would *atone* for the sins of the people. (Read about this in the 16th chapter of Leviticus.)

It was most likely William Tyndale, an English reformer who translated scripture into English, who coined our word *atonement*. It is also possible that *atonement* is the only theological word that is not based on an original language from the Bible. *Atonement* quite literally means "to bring into harmony" (to be "at one"—at + one, of course!). The English for *Yom Kippur* is Day of Atonement.

All right, so why is this cover, the *kapporeth*, called a "mercy seat" in English translations of the Bible? We can thank the reformer Martin Luther for that. When he was translating the Bible into the language of the people, in typical German fashion, he took the German word for "grace" (**Gnade**) and coupled it with "chair" (**Stuhl**), and the new compound word was **Gnadenstuhl**. Makes one wonder why the English was not given the literal translation: grace chair! Thanks be to God!

"When Moses went into the tent of meeting to speak with the LORD, he would hear the voice speaking to him from above the mercy seat that was on the ark of the covenant from between the two cherubim; thus it spoke to him." Numbers 7:89

One That Bites

"Now the serpent was more crafty than any other wild animal that the LORD God had made. He said to the woman, 'Did God say, "You shall not eat from any tree in the garden?"'" Genesis 3:1

Using just the clues from the verse, and not your personal opinion, what do we learn about the "serpent" in the verse above? It was *"crafty"* (*"shrewd"* in the Hebrew Bible). It was a *"wild animal"* and not a supernatural creature. It had been made by God, right along with the rest of creation! It was living in the garden, with all of the animals and the humans, all of which, not much earlier, had been found to be "good" and had been blessed by God. It is never called *"Satan"* or "the devil". In Hebrew, not even the word "serpent" is used; in fact, the word is **nahash**, which means *"one that bites"*.

Serpents also play a part in a curious story found in the book of Numbers:

The Israelites *"set out by the way to the Sea of Reeds, to go around the land of Edom; but the people became impatient on the way. The people spoke against God and against Moses, 'Why have you brought us up out of Egypt to die in the wilderness? For there is no food and no water, and we detest this miserable food.' Then the LORD sent poisonous serpents among the people, and they bit the people, so that many Israelites died. The people came to Moses and said, 'We have sinned against the LORD and against you; pray to the LORD to take away the serpents form us.' So Moses prayed for the people. And the LORD said to Moses, 'Make a poisonous serpent, and set it on a pole; and everyone who is bitten shall look at it and live.' So Moses made a serpent of bronze, and put it upon a pole; and whenever a serpent bit someone, that person would look at the serpent of bronze and live."* (Numbers 21:4-9)

Although the serpents in this tale are called *poisonous*, the Hebrew Bible has the word *fiery*, and interestingly, the word for *fiery* or *burning* is **seraph**. That has led some to very mistakenly assume that the angels known as **seraphim** must be winged snakes!

Moses' bronze serpent-on-a-stick evidently travels throughout the wilderness sojourn with the Israelites, because it ends up in Solomon's Temple, where many years later, King Hezekiah decided some reforms were needed:

"He broke in pieces the bronze serpent that Moses had made, for until those days the people of Israel had made offerings to it; it was called Nehushtan." (2 Kings 18:4) Nehushtan is "the one who bites".

So, what's going on in the Numbers story? Could it be as simple as telling the people to face their fears head-on instead of complaining? Beware of the ones that bite! Thanks be to God!

"Jesus answered…'And I, when I am lifted up from the earth, will draw all people to myself.'" John 12:32

Symbol of Seventy

"Your ancestors went down to Egypt seventy persons." Deuteronomy 10:22

Although the number 70 does not appear as frequently throughout scriptures, it, like 40 and 10 described elsewhere in these essays, is also a symbolic number. First, a quick tutorial on the basic building blocks of number symbolism!

We begin with the divine number, three. The Holy Trinity might be the first three-some that comes to mind, the Triune God consisting of Father, Son, and Holy Spirit. The holy name of God, found in Exodus 3:13-15, has three tenses of being. There are three facets of the **Shema**, recited by observant Jews: *"You shall love the LORD your God with all your heart, and with all your soul, and with all your might." (Deuteronomy 6:5)* Three annual festivals required pilgrimages to Jerusalem for all able-bodied males (Leviticus 23). Then, there is that recurring phrase, *"On the third day..."*! Can you find other uses of "three" in the Bible?

Next up, the number four, the earthly number. We have four seasons, we have four cardinal directions. Four rivers watered the garden of Eden (Genesis 2:10-14). The book of Revelation names *"four corners of the earth"* (Revelation 20:8). The books of Ezekiel and Revelation name four "living" creatures. The books of Zechariah and Revelation name four "horsemen".

If we add the divine and the earthly numbers, we arrive at seven, the number of completion or perfection. Sevens abound in the Bible! Seven days for creation; Sabbatical rest every seventh year for the land; seven sets of objects in Joseph's dreams; seven loaves and fishes, among other sets, including an amazing number of "sevens" to be found in the book of Revelation! Passover lasts seven days for the Jews. Roman Catholics have seven deadly sins, seven virtues, and seven sacraments.

That brings us to our topic: seventy, obviously the product of (7) the perfect number times (10), which is the number of human completeness (discussed in a separate essay). Whenever we find 70 in the Bible, we can assume it represents a full dimension of human completeness:

+The table of all (70) nations, given in Genesis 10:1-32;
+Jacob's family who ended up in Egypt (Genesis 46:27);
+The elders who served with Moses (Exodus 24:1, Numbers 11:16);
+And in the New Testament, *"After this the Lord appointed seventy others and sent them on ahead of him in pairs to every town and place where he himself intended to go." (Luke 10:1)*.

Seventy also suggests the full dimension of forgiveness. First, for the transgressions, Jeremiah reports, *"This whole land shall become a ruin and a waste, and these nations shall serve the king of Babylon seventy years." (Jeremiah 25:11)* Then, the restoration: *"For thus says the LORD: 'Only when Babylon's seventy years are completed will I visit you and I will fulfill to you my promise and bring you back to this place.'" (Jeremiah 29:10)*

Obviously the book of Jeremiah was read by Daniel: *"I, Daniel, perceived in the books the number of years that, according to the word of the LORD to the prophet Jeremiah, must be fulfilled for the devastation of Jerusalem, namely, seventy years." (Daniel 9:2)* Then, *"Seventy weeks are decreed for your people and your holy city: to finish the transgression, to put an end to sin, and to atone for iniquity, to bring in everlasting righteousness, to seal both vision and prophet, and to anoint a most holy place." (Daniel 9:24)*

As the Lord forgives, so must we, according to the Gospel of Matthew: *"Then Peter came and said to him, 'Lord, if my brother sins against me, how often should I forgive? As many as seven times?' Jesus said to him, 'Not seven times, but I tell you, seventy times.'" (Matthew 18:21-22)* Thanks be to God! And, one last thought:

"The days of our life are seventy years..." Psalm 90:10

Songs of Deliverance

"Hannah prayed and said, 'My heart exults in the LORD; my strength is exalted in my God...There is no Holy One like the LORD, no one besides you; there is no Rock like our God...The bows of the mighty are broken, but the feeble gird on strength...The LORD makes the poor and makes rich; he brings low, he also exalts...For the pillars of the earth are the LORD's, and on them he has set the world.'" 1 Samuel 2:1-10 excerpts

The book of Psalms, found near the center of the Bible, is the songbook of the Hebrew people. Psalms were an important part of their worship liturgy. But there are other songs included throughout the Bible; these are called "***canticles***". A small, but important, genre amidst the canticles are the "songs of deliverance", such as that excerpted above.

This canticle, a ***Magnificat***, is sung by Hannah to rejoice in her being granted a child. Note the themes that pervade this song: lifting up the lowly, bringing down the mighty, and praising God for his faithful strength. If this sounds familiar, you will certainly recognize the "lyrics" of this next canticle: *"My soul magnifies the Lord, and my spirit rejoices in God my Savior, for he has looked with favor on the lowliness of his servant. Surely, from now on all generations will call me blessed."* Any guesses? This is the opening of the *Magnificat* sung by Mary, at the news she will be the mother of the Son of God. It is found in Luke 1:46-55. Mary's canticle repeats the expected themes of Hannah's canticle: *"He has brought down the powerful from their thrones, and lifted up the lowly."* (Luke 1:52)

The canticle of Mary is sung regularly in the vespers or evening prayer services of the Lutheran and Episcopal churches, and it is an option in the matins or morning prayer liturgies. There is evidence in 1 Samuel 18:6-7 that the regular role of women was to sing during any victory celebrations, so these "songs of deliverance" are typical.

Scholars think that the very oldest portion of our Bible is the Song of Deliverance found in Judges 5. This is attributed to Deborah, one of the important leaders during the time of the Judges. With similar themes of bringing down the mighty and lifting up the lowly, this canticle tells of the bravery of the woman Jael, who single-handedly wins a victory against the enemy of the people.

The first canticle to be encountered in the chronology of the Bible is found in the 15th chapter of Exodus. God has just separated the sea, and the Israelites, departing from Egyptian bondage, cross on dry land, but the pursuing Egyptian chariots will be lost as the sea closes back upon them. Verse 1 suggests Moses led the song, but that is an editorial addition! In truth, we learn in the 21st verse who led the song: *"And Miriam sang to them: 'Sing to the LORD, for he has triumphed gloriously; horse and rider, he has thrown into the sea."* In verses 2-18, you will recognize the themes mentioned.

The ancients imagined that music echoed through the celestial spheres. As you read through the lyrics of Miriam's "Song of the Sea", you can almost hear an angelic choir joining in:
"Who is like you, O LORD, among the gods?
Who is like you, majestic in holiness, awesome in splendor, doing wonders?
…In your steadfast love you led the people whom you redeemed;
you guided them by your strength to your holy abode…
The LORD will reign forever and ever." Exodus 15:11-18

Anyone who has ever heard Handel's *Messiah* and has been drawn irresistibly to join in the *Hallelujah Chorus* knows how songs can stir the hearts of humanity. Jewish tradition claims that Miriam's canticle is the first time God received a song of praise…and he liked it! Thanks be to God!

"Hear, O kings; give ear, O princes; to the LORD I will sing,
I will make melody to the LORD, the God of Israel." Judges 5:3

The Glory of the Lord

"Moses and Aaron entered the tent of meeting, and then came out and blessed the people; and the glory of the LORD appeared to all the people. Fire came out from the LORD and consumed the burnt offering and the fat on the altar; and when all the people saw it, they shouted and fell on their faces." Leviticus 9:23-24

When we think of "glory", our likely tendency is to think of it paired with "fame", right? Fame and glory! In our 21st century American culture, those individuals to whom we ascribe fame and glory are the pop culture heroes. Sadly those are predominantly movie stars, maybe a few sports heroes could be thrown in as well. That's certainly not the glory we read about in the Bible!

In truth, when we read "glory" in the Old Testament, we may be missing out on the nuances available in Hebrew, because there are several Hebrew words that are regularly translated as "glory" in English.

For example, **hadar** means majesty or glory (*"Enter into the rock, and hide in the dust from the terror of the LORD, and from the glory of his majesty." Isaiah 2:10); **tohar** means brightness or glory; **ho'ah** means grandeur or glory (*"Deck yourself with majesty and dignity; clothe yourself with glory and splendor." Job 40:10)*; and, **kabod** also means glory.

The most frequently written in the Old Testament is **kabod**, which includes aspects of all the other words for glory, but when it is used in the Hebrew Bible, it is not translated into English as glory! It's too bad the English versions of the Bible do not follow the usage of their Hebrew cousins, because in the English translation of the Jewish Bible, the word *kabod* is always written as: *"The Very Presence of God"*!

Later Judaism uses the word **Shekhinah** to denote *The Very Presence of God,* but *Shekhinah* does not appear in the Bible. Rabbinic tradition holds that whenever men are gathered to study the Torah, the *Shekhinah* is considered to be present. Many theologians connect *Shekhinah* with the Greek New Testament concept, **parousia**, which also means *Presence.* We get a glimpse of the rabbinic tradition about gathering in Matthew 18:20: *"For where two or three are gathered in my name, I am there among them."*

The Gospel of John narrates stories of Jesus performing seven "signs of glory" (**doxa** in Greek), beginning with the Wedding at Cana and ending with the raising of Lazarus. These are never called miracles, because that words hints too much at magic. No, signs of glory are glimpses of what God's intentions are for abundant living. They are intersections of the divine with the human. Have you witnessed examples of this in your life? Thanks be to God!

"In the year that King Uzziah died, I saw the Lord sitting on a throne, high and lofty; and the hem of his robe filled the temple. Seraphs were in attendance above him; each had six wings….And one called to another and said: 'Holy, holy, holy is the LORD of hosts; the whole earth is full of his glory.'" Isaiah 6:1-3

Everlasting Covenant

"I will establish my covenant between me and you, and your offspring after you throughout their generations, for an everlasting covenant, to be God to you and to your offspring after you." Genesis 17:7

In story after story in the book of Genesis, we encounter flawed characters and dysfunctional families. Indeed, the persistence of human sin might be the most permeating motif throughout the Bible. (1 John 1:8-9: *"If we say we have no sin, we deceive ourselves and the truth is not in us."*) But if sin is ubiquitous in the Bible, so is God's activity in dealing with it.

In story after story, beginning in the book of Genesis, the testimony of the Bible is that God approaches individuals to enter into relationship. The term for this divine-human relationship is *covenant.*

There are many Biblical examples of alliances between humans, including contracts, treaties, and marriages. The Hebrew word for covenant originally meant "shackle" or "chain". But the Biblical concept of covenant as relationship with God is something new and marvelous. The novel element is that mortal humans would be bound into a relationship in which God, the Creator of the Universe, is a party in the promises! For the Jewish people, the covenant with God introduced in Genesis is **Berit Olam**, which translates as "Everlasting Covenant".

We find a foundation for covenant in God's three-fold promise to Abram (Abraham) in Genesis 12:2-3: *"I will make of you a great nation, and make your name great, so that you will be a blessing…in you all the families of the earth shall be blessed."* As we keep reading in Genesis, each of these promises is elevated to a covenant, which we find fulfilled later in Scripture.

The promise of nationhood, ratified in Genesis 15, we see fulfilled in the Mosaic Covenant, when the "family" is forged into a nation during its experiences under Moses' leadership in the wilderness for forty years. The promise of a great name, ratified in Genesis 17, will be fulfilled in the Davidic Covenant, the continuation of King David's dynasty. The promise of worldwide blessing, ratified in

Genesis 22, comes to fruition with the New Covenant, which is the universal blessing poured out with Christ's blood.

So, two little Hebrew words, *Berit Olam*, summarize all of God's saving action…and we are confident that God's promise, this covenant, is valid in perpetuity. For ever and ever…Amen. Thanks be to God!

"I hereby make a covenant. Before all your people I will perform marvels, such as have not been performed in all the earth or in any nation; and all the people among whom you live shall see the work of the LORD; for it is an awesome thing that I will do with you." Exodus 34:10

Sabbath

"So God blessed the seventh day and hallowed it, because on it God rested from all the work that he had done in creation." Genesis 2:3

"Remember the sabbath day, and keep it holy. For six days you shall labor and do all your work. But the seventh day is a sabbath to the LORD your God; you shall not do any work—you, your son or your daughter, your male or female slave, your livestock, or the alien resident in your towns. For in six days the LORD made heaven and earth, the sea, and all that is in them, but rested the seventh day; therefore the Lord blessed the sabbath day and consecrated it." Exodus 20:8-11

Most of us believe that the first time we find the word "Sabbath" in the Bible is in the story of creation in Genesis. But check out the first verse quoted above...is it there? Not in English! Rest assured, however, it does appear in the Hebrew Bible. The word is **Shabbat**. Even though we do read the word "rested" in English, the actual intention in the passage is that this is a cessation rather than a rest-period. God ceased working because creation was accomplished, not because he was tired.

The commandment shown from the Exodus passage quoted above, is actually the longest one of the *Decalogue*. We know that observance of the Sabbath was a cornerstone of the Israelite religious practice from the earliest times, an observance well regulated by the Levite tribe of priests. For people who had been slaves for centuries in Egypt and later in Babylonia, the idea of a day each week of resting from their labors was a unique and liberating gift from God. Yes, rest from work is important, but is that the most important idea behind the Sabbath?

Whenever the people ceased from work, they ceased from worldliness, right? This was a way to keep HOLY! It was a regular, recurring reminder that they belonged to God, as they were separated from the rest of the world. This marked them as holy people.

When the people were in exile in Babylonia, they no longer had the Temple as central in their midst. With the Temple demolished, they had to ask themselves, "Where do we find God *now*?" They formerly had believed God dwelt inside the Temple...within the Holy of Holies, that most sacred space. Observing the Sabbath taught them that God is not relegated to a particular space. No, God can also be found in time, a holy time set aside each week.

When we read the story of the covenant between God and Israel, as expressed in the story in Exodus, we learn that even though circumcision was a sign of the covenant between God and Abraham and his male descendants, there is now a new sign of the covenant between God and the people: *"The LORD said to Moses: You yourself are to speak to the Israelites; 'You shall keep my Sabbaths, for this is a sign between me and you throughout your generations, given in order that you may know that I, the LORD, sanctify you. You shall keep the Sabbath because it is holy for you. …Therefore the Israelites shall keep the Sabbath, observing the Sabbath throughout their generations, as a perpetual covenant. It is a sign forever between me and the people of Israel…'"* (Exodus 31:12-14, 16-17)

So, the Sabbath is much more than just a day off from work! It is meant to be a day off—or time off—from worldliness and given over to holiness. At the root of the word *Shabbat* is the number seven. Is it possible to re-align our understanding of Sabbath by considering that number? Should it only be 1/7 of each week given over to holiness? Why not 1/7 of each day? Or 1/7 of each hour? You get the idea. Thanks be to God!

"The Lord spoke to Moses on Mount Sinai, saying, 'Speak to the people of Israel and say to them: When you enter the land that I am giving you, the land shall observe a sabbath for the LORD. For six years you shall sow your field, and for six years you shall prune your vineyard, and gather in their yield; but in the seventh year there shall be a sabbath of complete rest for the land, a sabbath for the LORD.'" Leviticus 25:1-7

The Face of God

"The LORD bless you and keep you;
the LORD make his face to shine upon you, and be gracious to you;
the LORD lift up his countenance upon you, and give you peace." Numbers 6:24-
26

Let's take a look at another word that shows up in various ways throughout the Torah, and that is "face". The word "face" is, of course, used literally in the Bible, in passages such as: *"Then Abram fell on his face." (Genesis 17:3)* In the passage above, it is used anthropomorphically, assigning human qualities to God.   The Hebrew word for face is **panim**. The same word also translates to "countenance", so *panim* is actually found twice in the Numbers verses above.

Because the human face reflects moods and emotions, one's "countenance" can often be read in one's *panim*. For example, when Cain noted that the Lord did not have regard for his offering but preferred the offering of his brother Abel, we are told Cain's "countenance" fell (Genesis 4:5). God perceives this change of face and warns Cain to behave himself!

Much later in Genesis, we find an interesting use of *panim*. When Jacob is returning to his homeland after spending many years away, he was quite worried that his brother Esau would still be holding a grudge against him for tricking their father out of his deathbed blessing. He was so worried that he had restless night. During the night, an unknown man showed up and wrestled with Jacob until daybreak; the full story is in Genesis 32:22-32. We are given clues that Jacob may have been wrestling with a divine being. When the sun rose in the morning, Jacob said, *"For I have seen God face to face, and yet my life is preserved." (Genesis 32:30)*

Prior to the all-night wrestling match, Jacob had been fearful of meeting his brother again face to face. The next morning, when the brothers do face each other, Esau embraces and kisses Jacob, and the brothers wept. Jacob tells Esau, *"For truly to see your face is like seeing the face of God—since you have received me with such favor." (Genesis 33:10)* Why would Jacob describe the encounter this way? Esau's welcome was a sign of forgiveness, and this meant God's promises were being carried forward.

Another usage for *panim* is found in the 25th chapter of Exodus, where Moses is given instructions for furnishing the Ark of the Covenant, which will hold very holy objects. One of these items is a table on which the "Bread of the Presence" is to be kept. This holy bread was always to be kept in this sanctuary. This was not ordinary bread. There were to be twelve loaves (one for each of the tribes), and they would be arranged on a table of pure gold, as an offering to the Lord: *"Every sabbath day Aaron shall set them in order before the LORD regularly as a commitment of the people of Israel, as a covenant forever." (Leviticus 24:8)*

Here is the fascinating bit about this bread. As a sign of the covenant, it was a sign of God's continued presence, but the literal translation for Bread of Presence is "Bread of the *Face*" *(panim)*. The people were meant to see this as a visible sign of God's face. Tradition was that at the pilgrim festival of Pentecost (celebrating the fiftieth day in the wilderness when the people were given the gift of the commandments), the priests would elevate the Bread of the Face before all the people and say, "BEHOLD GOD'S LOVE FOR YOU!" God's Face, God's Presence, a visible sign of God's love! Thanks be to God!

"For truly to see your face is like seeing the face of God—since you have received me with such favor." Genesis 33:10

Bless and Curse

"If you will only obey the LORD your God, by diligently observing all his commandments that I am commanding you today, the LORD your God will set you high above all the nations of the earth; all these blessings shall come upon you and overtake you, if you obey the LORD your God." Deuteronomy 28:1-2

"But if you will not obey the LORD your God by diligently observing all his commandments and decrees, which I am commanding you today, then all these curses shall come upon you and overtake you." Deuteronomy 28:15

These two passages are just a brief taste of the 28th chapter in Deuteronomy, where Moses is giving the people instruction as to how the covenant with God will be ratified as soon as they have crossed the River Jordan into the promised land of Canaan. Half of the tribes of Israel are to ascend Mt Ebal, while the other half of the tribes will ascend Mt Gerizim. Then a detailed lists of blessings and curses are shouted out across the valley, with the people all shouting "Amen."

There is support in Joshua 8:30-35 that such a ceremony did take place, and it included all the men, "and the women, and the little children" climbing up either Mt Ebal or Mt Gerizim, according to the instructions Moses had given. This is called the *Shechem Ceremony.*

The blessings and curses coincide with either following or not following the covenant with God. Contrary to our modern understanding of "curse", however, the curses are not a description of divine punishment for disobeying the commands, and neither are the blessings rewards for compliance.

The Hebrew word ***barak***, that is translated as "bless", literally means to "kneel down". This concept suggests that *barak* involves offering something or doing something for another. By extension, *barak* means that God will provide for our needs, and our part of the bargain is to give ourselves to God.

It may be helpful to remember the child-rearing advice of the 1980's, to use natural and logical consequences rather than punishments and rewards to motivate children toward appropriate behavior. God, our Father, has given the gift of instructions for harmonious living. If we follow this way of life, we can be assured that we are serving God. If we elect to disregard the instructions, however, our contrary behavior tends to set into motion results, or consequences, that are not harmonious. Such disharmony can have long-reaching impact, but God does not cause it or desire it.

The benedictions and maledictions found in Deuteronomy 27 & 28 may remind you of a familiar passage from Luke's Gospel; check out Luke 6:20-26. The *"blessed are you's"* and *"woe to you's"* that Jesus offers in this sermon are, again, statements describing natural consequences. They most certainly are not proclamations actively separating people into camps of ever-lasting salvation versus eternal damnation. *"Blessed"*, as used here in Luke, is a description and not a prediction. *"Woe"* is a word that means *"Alas!"*.

Benedictions and maledictions are descriptions of how things are. God desires to shower his blessings upon his children. Let's not be strong-willed and contrary children. Thanks be to God!

"For you bless the righteous, O LORD;
you cover them with favor as with a shield." Psalm 5:12

To Judge or Not to Judge

"May the LORD therefore be judge, and give sentence between me and you. May he see to it, and plead my cause, and vindicate me against you." 1 Samuel 24:15

For English speakers, the word *judge* has one connotation; it only suggests a court-like or judiciary action. Usually one party hears a case between two other parties in conflict; the judge then judges which party is in the right and what is to be done about it.

That is certainly the case in Genesis 16:5: *"Then Sarai said to Abram, 'May the wrong done to me be on you! I gave my slave-girl to your embrace, and when she saw that she had conceived, she looked on me with contempt. May the LORD judge between you and me!'"* The Hebrew word that translates as "judge" here is **sapat**.

But *sapat* is rich with definitions. Not always is it used in a judicial sense. Other functions that can be called *sapat* include leadership roles of a political or a military nature. Sometimes it means any process whereby law and order are maintained.

In the verse above quoted from 1 Samuel, there is a twist. The word that is translated from *sapat* is not "judge", it is "vindicate"! *Sapat* can just as often describe deliverance from oppression or injustice as any other definition. That is the sense of *sapat* as it is found in the book of Judges. In fact, a better title for the seventh book of the Bible would be "Deliverers". The men and women we meet in this book do not sit in courtroom-like judgment upon anyone; rather, they deliver their people from injustice and oppression.

Check out some of the short stories within the book, and you will meet some vivid characters: the left-handed Ehud (chapter 3), the fearless ladies Deborah and Jael (chapter 4), young Gideon (chapter 6), and strong-man Samson (chapters 13 through16). Each rose up when needed and delivered their people.

Maybe this alternative will give you something to ponder the next time you recite the Apostles' Creed. What would it mean if *"judge"* were changed to *"deliver"*? *"He will come again to judge the living and the dead."* Thanks be to God!

"Then the LORD raised up judges who delivered them out of the power of those who plundered them." Judges 2:16

My Redeemer

"I know that my Redeemer lives." Job 19:25

Some of us might recognize this sentence as the opening lyrics of a Christian hymn found in most church hymnals and frequently sung at Easter. Even more folks would identify this as one of the pieces in the great oratorio written in 1741 by George Frideric Handel: *"Messiah"*. In both instances the "Redeemer" who lives is undoubtedly Jesus Christ.

There are a couple of surprising things about the title "Redeemer". First, it is not found even once in the entire New Testament. Second, it is found in the Old Testament but never referring to Jesus Christ.

The Hebrew word that is translated into redeemer is ***go'el***. But sometimes *go'el* is translated as "kinsman" or "next-of-kin", which is the case in the beautiful book of Ruth in the Old Testament. The short story tells the tale of Ruth, a widow, who asks a near relative of her husband to act as *go'el*, which will involve marrying her. Naturally the man, Boaz, agrees, and the couple becomes the great-grandparents for future King David.

In the complex legal codes of Leviticus, Numbers, and Deuteronomy, the duties of a *go'el* are addressed, in cases involving relatives experiencing serfdom, slavery, widowhood, injury, or death. The *go'el* is the nearest of kin who is to take the responsibility of vindicating the helpless relative.

The reassuring nature of *go'el* shines forth in its usage throughout Isaiah. The great prophet casts God as the redeemer for his people:

"Thus says the LORD, the King of Israel,
and his Redeemer, the LORD of hosts:
I am the first and I am the last;
besides me there is no god.
Who is like me?
Let them proclaim it,
Let them declare and set it forth before me.

91

Who has announced from of old the things to come?
Let them tell us what is yet to be.
Do not fear, or be afraid;
Have I not told you from of old and declared it?
You are my witnesses!
Is there any god besides me?
There is no other rock; I know not one." (Isaiah 44:6-8)

So, when we read in the various Isaiah passages about God as the Redeemer, we must apply the Hebrew definition for the word *go'el.* That, of course, is the next-of-kin. Isaiah reassures his listeners that God, the Redeemer of Israel, will redeem the people from their captivity.

God is identifying himself as our closest relative. What could be more reassuring than that idea? God is our nearest relative (*"Our Father", "Abba", "Daddy"!),* a kinsman who accepts the role of *go'el* for us, the one who accepts the duty of righting the wrongs and restoring us. Thanks be to God!

"They remembered that God was their rock,
the Most High God their redeemer." Psalm 78:35

The Satan

"One day the heavenly beings came to present themselves before the LORD, and the Accuser also came among them to present himself before the LORD. The LORD said to the Accuser, 'Where have you come from?' The Accuser answered the LORD, 'From going to and fro on the earth, and from walking up and down on it.'" Job 2:1-2

As you read this start to the familiar tale of Job, you may be wondering whom this *"Accuser"* could be. Maybe you have read a translation that substitutes the word *"Satan"* instead. Both *"Accuser"* and *"Satan"* are accurate for the text. In the Hebrew original, the word was **"ha-satan"**, which translates as *"the Accuser"* or *"the Adversary"*. The definite article *"the"* is very much a part of the translation. *"Satan"* is not the first name of any being to be found in the Old Testament. Nor is the word *"devil"* used.

The book of Job is a very ancient story, and the plot begins with the Lord speaking to one of the members of a divine council. As explained in the story, this *ha-satan* is sort of an independent prosecutor, who suggests that Job is only a blameless and upright individual because God has blessed him so richly. The *ha-satan* then undertakes to prove this to God.

Of the 23,145 verses in the Old Testament, apart from this opening prologue in Job, *ha-satan* is used just two more times. One of these is in the 3rd chapter of the minor prophet Zechariah:
"Then he showed me the high priest Joshua standing before the angel of the LORD, and the Adversary standing at his right hand to accuse him. And the LORD said to the Adversary, 'The LORD rebuke you, O Adversary!'" (Zechariah 3:1-2) Again, *ha-satan* is "the *Adversary*", acting very like a prosecuting attorney.

The only other use of *ha-satan* is 1 Chronicles 21:1, where we read, *"Satan stood up against Israel, and incited David to count the people of Israel. So David said to Joab and the commanders of the army, 'Go, number Israel…and bring me a report, so that I may know their number.'"*

The point is that even though there is lots of sinning going on throughout the Old Testament, no one could ever say, "The devil made me do it." Nothing in 23,140 verses identifies a supernatural enemy of mankind named Satan who can wrench us from the embrace of God. Thanks be to God!

"Those who render me evil for good
are my adversaries because I follow after good." Psalm 38:20

The Anointed One

"The spirit of the Lord God is upon me, because the LORD *has anointed me; he has sent me to bring good news to the oppressed, to bind up the brokenhearted, to proclaim liberty to the captive, and release to the prisoners; to proclaim the year of the* LORD's *favor..." Isaiah 61:1-2*

If you were to search a concordance of the Bible, you might be surprised that the word *Messiah* does not appear in the Old Testament. The Hebrew word, **mashiach**, is translated instead as *"anointed one"*. We call that a *Messiah*, but the English Old Testament does not. And when *Messiah* appears in the New Testament, we are actually reading the English rendition of the Greek word **Christos**, which means...any guesses? *The anointed one.* In neither Testament does the word equate with *Savior.*

Anointing, in the Old Testament, was done for consecration, which was a setting apart, for a special job or function. The high priest would have been anointed (Leviticus 4:3). Kings would have been anointed (1 Samuel 10:1; 1 Kings 1:39). Prophets, too, would be anointed (1 Kings 19:15-16).

Observant Jews recite a particular prayer called the **Amidah** three times each day. One of the petitions is for a *Messiah* to come. Since the Jews do not believe this has yet happened, there have been, historically, differing hopes for what a *Messiah* would do exactly.

One such model would be a political messiah, maybe a king or a warrior, who could bring God's liberation, relying on God's law. Another model would be a prophetic messiah, who would bring God's restoration, through proclaiming words of truth. There is also a priestly model, a messiah who could make atonement or reconciliation with God, especially through sacrifice.

It is interesting that one of the biggest storylines in the Old Testament is that of the Exodus, with leading man Moses as God's mediator. The people were in bondage, but God, through Moses, liberates them from slavery to Sabbath. A second big storyline in the Old Testament is that of the Exile, with all the prophets as God's mediators, speaking God's truth that when the people stray from the covenant, an ever-faithful God will restore them to their homeland. The New Testament has one storyline: the Good News of Jesus, Emmanuel, who offers the ultimate atonement for all to be reconciled with God.

If we take the characters from these three storylines, Jesus, Moses, and let's say Elijah for the prophet, there is a fascinating intersection of all three in the story of the Transfiguration (Matthew 17:1-8, Mark 9:2-8, Luke 9:28-36). Transfiguration is from a Greek word that means transformation. The three disciples who witnessed this saw Jesus transformed before their very eyes; Jesus' face shone like the sun, and dazzling white light radiated from his clothing. It is as if all the storylines are coalesced into one intersection of the human and the divine at the Transfiguration. *Messiah* might be an elusive word in the Old Testament, but the New Testament leaves no doubt. Thanks be to God!

"Now I know that the LORD will help his anointed;
he will answer him from his holy heaven
with mighty victories by his right hand.
Some take pride in chariots,
And some in horses,
But our pride is in the name of the LORD our God." Psalm 20:6-7

Release to the Captives

"The spirit of the Lord GOD is upon me, because the LORD has anointed me; he has sent me to bring good news to the oppressed, to bind up the brokenhearted, to proclaim liberty to the captives, and release to the prisoners; to proclaim the year of the LORD's favor." Isaiah 61:1-2

What is this year of the Lord's favor that Isaiah mentions? To find out, we need to go back to the Torah, particularly the 25th chapter of Leviticus. Moses had been commanded by God that once the people were residing in Canaan, the *"land shall observe a Sabbath for the LORD"*. We know that observing a Sabbath day every week was a perpetual sign of the covenant for the people (Exodus 31:12). For the land, a Sabbath meant six years of working the land and then one year of *"complete rest for the land"*. (Leviticus 25:1-7)

That's not all! Every Hebrew indentured servant who had worked for six years was to receive manumission in the seventh year (Deuteronomy 15:12). Slaves, too, were to go free in the seventh year, after serving for six years (Exodus 21:2). That's not even all! *"Every seventh year you shall grant a remission of debts."* *(Deuteronomy 15:1)* Isn't that something!

When Jesus begins his ministry in the gospel of Luke, the first thing we read is that he went into the synagogue in Nazareth, and he was handed the scroll of Isaiah to read. The passage he read was Isaiah 61:1-2, the text quoted above. Jesus then said, *"Today this scripture has been fulfilled in your hearing."* *(Luke 4:21)* How? We know that Jesus' ministry consisted of forgiving people and healing people. We also know that he got into trouble with the Jewish leaders because he tended to do this on the Sabbath day.

If Jesus' healings were only about physical health, they could have occurred on any day of the week. Jesus goes out of his way to heal on the Sabbath. Why? The essence of the Sabbath as a day of "rest" also has connotations of "rest" from any sort of debt. Just as the concept of a sabbatical year included release from bondage and forgiveness of debts, Jesus is reclaiming the Sabbath day. He is releasing people from their bondage to sin.

The concept of the sabbatical year gets even better, according to Leviticus. Every seven sets of seven years, there would be a bonus. The fiftieth year was called the **Jubilee** year. The name comes from the Hebrew word **Yovel**. A *yovel* was a blast from the trumpet made from a ram's horn, a **yobhel** in Hebrew. This trumpet was called a **shofar**.

The Jubilee year included all of the remissions of the sabbatical and more. All property was to be returned to the original owner or heir. (Leviticus 25:13-17) The idea behind this is that the people could only ever be tenants. Land could not be sold forever, because land did not belong to anyone except the Lord! This is a strong reminder of just how much is from God.

On July 8, 1776, a famous bell rang to summon people to hear a reading of the Declaration of Independence. Inscribed upon the Liberty Bell are these words from Leviticus: *"Proclaim LIBERTY throughout all the land unto all the inhabitants thereof. Lev. XXV v. X"*. Thanks be to God!

"And you shall hallow the fiftieth year and you shall proclaim liberty throughout the land to all its inhabitants. It shall be a jubilee for you; you shall return, every one of you, to your property and every one of you to your family." Leviticus 25:10

The Fourth Cup

"Say therefore to the Israelites, 'I am the LORD, and I will free you from the burdens of the Egyptians and deliver you from slavery to them. I will redeem you with an outstretched arm and with mighty acts of judgment. I will take you as my people, and I will be your God.'" Exodus 6:6-7

If you have ever attended a Passover Seder meal, you know how very regulated they are. One of the components of the organized remembrance is the compulsory four cups of wine. The meal begins with the first cup, the *Cup of Sanctification*. After that a plateful of symbolic foods are presented, including bitter herbs, haroseth, and roasted lamb.

The tradition of the four cups arose from the Exodus passage quoted above. Within the verses, notice that God announces four mighty acts that he will accomplish for his people: he *will free* them, he *will deliver* them, he *will redeem* them, and he *will take* them as his own. Each of these mighty acts is the basis for a cup of wine.

The second cup, the *Cup of Proclamation* is taken before the children ask, "Why is this night different?" When the responses, all from scripture, to the questions are given, participants give thanks again and sing specific psalms. After the dinner has been eaten, the third cup, the *Cup of Blessing* is taken. Then more psalms are sung. The Passover meal is complete after the fourth cup, the *Cup of Praise*, is taken.

With this outline of a seder meal in mind, consider the gospel account of Jesus' last supper: *"When the hour came, he took his place at the table, and the apostles with him. He said to them, 'I have eagerly desired to eat this Passover with you before I suffer; for I tell you, I will not eat it until it is fulfilled in the kingdom of God.' Then he took a cup, and after giving thanks he said, 'Take this and divide it among yourselves; for I tell you that from now on I will not drink of the fruit of the vine until the kingdom of God comes.' Then he took a loaf of bread, and when he had given thanks, he broke it and gave it to them, saying, 'This is my body, which is given for you. Do this in remembrance of me.' And he did the same with the cup after supper, saying, 'This cup that is poured out for you is the new covenant in my blood.'" (Luke 22:14-20)*

One other important verse is included in Matthew's and Mark's versions: *"When they had sung the hymn, they went out to the Mount of Olives."* (Matthew 26:30, Mark 14:26) What have you noticed? Luke clearly mentions that it was after supper that Jesus took a cup. That means the other cup Luke identified must have been the *Cup of Proclamation*, the second cup. And notice that after that cup is offered, Jesus blessed the bread, offered it, and explained its meaning.

Rather than explaining the past Exodus from Egypt and the "body" of the Passover lamb, which a Jewish father would have done, instead Jesus identifies himself with the bread as his own "body". The cup of wine they had after the bread/body must be the third cup, the *Cup of Blessing*.

If we follow the Matthew and Mark versions at this point, we know Jesus and his disciples now sing a hymn—this must be the psalms! The texts never tell us that the fourth and final cup of wine is taken. Indeed, Jesus claims that he will not drink of the wine again until his kingdom has been fulfilled.

The next mention of a "cup" occurs in the next scene of the drama, the Mount of Olives, where Jesus prays. Do you remember that prayer? *"Father, if you are willing, remove this cup from me; yet, not my will but yours be done."* (Luke 22:42)

Could Jesus be speaking of the fourth cup, knowing that as soon as the fourth cup of the wine is consumed, the Passover liturgy is complete?

The gospels report that on the cross, Jesus is offered wine, mixed with myrrh, that he does not drink: *"And they offered him wine mixed with myrrh; but he did not take it."* (Mark 15:23)

Then, the hour had come: *"After this, when Jesus knew that all was now finished, he said (in order to fulfill the scripture), 'I am thirsty.' A jar full of sour wine was standing there. So they put a sponge full of the wine on a branch of hyssop and held it to his mouth. When Jesus had received the wine he said, 'It is finished.' Then he bowed his head and gave up his spirit."* (John 19:28-30)

Hyssop—a branch of the same was used to swipe the lamb's blood on the doorposts in Egypt (Exodus 12:22).

Jesus has taken his "last" drink of wine. What is now finished? His mission? His life? Could it be that now the Passover is finished, because he did drink the final cup. By extending his last Passover meal to include his death, Jesus has instituted a New Passover. Thanks be to God!

"Do this in remembrance of me." Luke 22:19

One-Year-Old Lamb without Blemish

"The LORD said to Moses, '...Tell the whole congregation of Israel that on the tenth of this month they are to take a lamb for each family... Your lamb shall be without blemish, a year-old male.'" Exodus 12:1,5

The instructions given to Moses in the book of Exodus for the Passover preparation specify that the sacrificial lamb must be a one-year-old lamb, without blemish. Keep that fact in mind.

Of the four gospel accounts of the life of Jesus in the New Testament, Matthew, Mark and Luke have great similarity. John, on the other hand, is markedly unique. John has no stories of Jesus' birth, no story of his baptism, no temptation account, no exorcisms, no parables, no Sermon on the Mount, no Lord's Prayer, and no Transfiguration. It does have lengthy stories that the other three gospels do not: the wedding at Cana, the woman at the well, the raising of Lazarus, the foot-washing of the disciples, and others.

There is more. Matthew, Mark and Luke are understood to show that the ministry of Jesus lasted only one year. Why do most people assume Jesus' ministry lasted three years? The reasoning is that the word "Passover" is brought up three times in John's gospel, suggesting to some that Jesus attended three separate Passovers during his ministry, which means three years.

A critical reading of John's gospel, however, will support the alternate possibility that it, too, describes only a one-year ministry. Throughout John, as Jesus' full year of ministry is described, the evangelist mentions Jesus attending in sequence a full year's worth of the Jewish festivals: Passover, the Festival of Weeks, the Festival of Booths, the Festival of Dedication, and a final Passover.

As Jesus and his disciples "walk" through this year of Jewish observances, Jesus' focus seems especially attuned to the particular traditions of each festival, in turn. For instance:

John's 5th chapter probably takes place during the Festival of Weeks, a spring harvest observance, when offerings of grain, particularly the first barley of the season, are given. In the very next chapter, Jesus is feeding a multitude from two loaves of barley bread and describing himself as the "bread of life".

John's 7th chapter is set during the Festival of Booths, when an elaborate water ritual is performed each day by the priests in the Temple. While pouring golden pitchers of water on the altar, prayers are given for restoration, with the expectation that the rivers that had watered the Garden of Eden would burst forth from the altar! At this time, Jesus begins to speak of rivers of living water, and he claims he is the new altar from which living water flows.

John's 10th chapter mentions the Festival of Dedication, which we know as Hanukkah, the Festival of Lights. In the previous two chapters, Jesus restores sight (which is to say light!) to a man born blind and claims to be the "light of the world".

Beginning in the 11th chapter, John's gospel refers the "approaching" Passover. (There had also been one reference in chapter 6 to "the Passover of the Jews being near".)

There is another important difference between John's gospel and the other three. John follows a different chronology for Jesus. For example, Matthew, Mark and Luke place the cleansing of the Temple in the last week of Jesus' life; whereas, John places it at the very start of his ministry rather than the last week!

The last clue is that only in John's gospel is the crucifixion of Jesus on a different day, the Day of Preparation for the Passover (John 19:14). According to the instructions given in the Torah, the Passover preparations are made the day before Passover. That is when the blemish-free one-year-old lambs are sacrificed.

Keep in mind that only in John's gospel had Jesus been called the "Lamb of God" (by John the Baptist). For the evangelist John, Jesus is the embodiment of the Paschal Lamb. Jesus' one year of ministry corresponds with the age of the sacrificial lambs, one year. When the gospel of John says the Passover was near, it refers to the new, symbolic Passover; it refers to Jesus himself!

Following the chronology of John's gospel, and following John's symbolic reinterpretation for the annual cycle of Jewish festivals, it is likely that the evangelist wants us to see that, along with the other Jewish festivals in the annual cycle, the Passover is being reinterpreted, metaphorically, with Jesus as the Paschal lamb, a lamb without blemish. Thanks be to God!

"Here is the Lamb of God who takes away the sin of the world." John 1:29

On the Third Day

"The LORD said to Moses: "Go to the people and consecrate them today and tomorrow. Have them wash their clothes and prepare for the third day, because on the third day the LORD will come down upon Mount Sinai in the sight of all the people." Exodus 19:10-11

Are you surprised that a Bible text from Exodus would emphasize "on the third day"? We are so used to our creedal proclamation formula ("On the third day he rose again...") that we probably assume it is always reference to what happened to Jesus on the third day after his crucifixion. And, we'd be right, except that is not the first instance in the Bible when the phrase occurs.

Actually the phrase "on the third day" occurs over 35 times in the Old Testament, and only a little over a dozen times in the New Testament! It is found a half dozen times in Genesis. The fact that it does occur so frequently suggests that we should look a little closer.

The first use, in Genesis 22:4, is in the story of Abraham taking his beloved son up Mt Moriah for a sacrifice; it is "on the third day" that he sees the place God had revealed. Its final use in Genesis (42:18) is when Joseph reveals part of his plan to his brothers, who, as yet, do not know who he is. A more amazing occurrence of the phrase is in the 19th chapter of Exodus. It is in this narrative that the Israelite nation, brought by Moses to the base of Mt Sinai, is about to experience God—a theophany of such atmospheric magnificence that every one of the 600,000 men (give or take a few thousands, according to Exodus) will witness the Very Presence of God being revealed to them. (The Ten Commandments are spoken in the next chapter.)

Check out what is revealed to David on the third day in 2 Samuel 1:2, or what day the Temple was rededicated (Ezra 6:14-16), or what Hosea prophesies in Hosea 6:2, or when the wedding of Cana occurred (John 2:1), or how long Saul was blinded after his vision of Jesus (Acts 9:9). It seems that "on the third day" alerts us to "a big reveal" (as the expression is used on television shows these days!).

If we know about number symbolism in the Bible, we are aware that the number three represents the divine. When we encounter "on the third day" in our readings of Scripture, we should be prepared to pay attention: God is about to do something amazing! Thanks be to God!

"After two days he will revive us; on the third day he will raise us up, that we may live before him." Hosea 6:2

And note how many times Jesus predicts what will occur on the third day:

+ *"From that time on, Jesus began to show his disciples that he must go to Jerusalem and undergo great suffering at the hands of the elders and chief priests and scribes, and be killed, and on the third day be raised." Matthew 16:21*

+ *"As they were gathering in Galilee, Jesus said to them, 'The Son of Man is going to be betrayed into human hands, and they will kill him, and on the third day he will be raised.'" Matthew 17:23*

+ *" 'See we are going up to Jerusalem, and the Son of Man will be handed over to the chief priests and scribes, and they will condemn him to death; then they will hand him over to the Gentiles to be mocked and flogged and crucified; and on the third day he will be raised.'" Matthew 20:19*

The Righteous One

*"You are righteous, O LORD,
and your judgments are right." Psalm 119:137*

The Hebrew gets complicated with the concept of righteousness! The adjective **tsaddiq** is used about God. Related nouns are **tsedeq** and **tsedaqah**. Not that *righteous* and *righteousness* are not good English equivalents, they are.

However, since the Hebrew words were first translated into Greek and later into Latin, our understanding for what righteousness means is colored by those words, which definitely carry a legalistic undertone: *just, justice, justification.*

Today our tendency, when applying the adjective to humans, is to combine the word with the prefix "self-", in an unflattering designation: *self-righteous.* We see *righteousness* as a perfection that humans just cannot attain. Only God has moral perfection.

Throughout the Old Testament, God is called *righteous* again and again. When viewed with a legalistic or ethical lens, we see God as the absolute law-giver and the absolute judge. *Tsaddiq* is not that static; there is more dynamic infusing its definition.

In the narratives we encounter in the Old Testament, what is often being described is God's righteousness in regard to the covenant with his people. When considered in that way, we would need to use adjectives that mean more than *goodness.* The important concept underlying *righteousness* is *relationship,* with expectations for faithfulness and loyalty and action. For humans, this means we strive to be in a right-relationship with God, in alignment with God. Meanwhile, God keeps working to bring us into this right-relationship.

Many people believe that if we obey God's laws, we will attain righteousness. Would you agree? The problem is that the teachings in the Torah, often called "the Law", instead show us how far we are from reaching any state of righteousness. The Torah/the Law is God's gift for an orderly existence, of how to live in harmony with God and

107

mankind, setting us apart as people of God. But, if left to our own devices, we only seem to manage disharmony.

The word *tsedaqah* is also used to describe God in Judges 5, in Deborah's *Song of Deliverance*. What these verses seem to express is the absolute conviction that God will put things right for God's people. What is fascinating is that various English translations of *tsedaqah* for the Judges passage include words like *triumphs, victories, righteous acts,* or *blessings*. This understanding of God's ultimate triumph or victory was the original understanding for the term "Day of the Lord", too. It was to be a day of God's vindication, when God would put things right through his own means.

By the time of the prophetic writings, when folks like Amos were unsure whether the Israelites could keep the responsibilities of being in covenant with God, "The Day of the Lord" came to mean a time of separating the good from the bad: *"Alas for you who desire the day of the LORD! …It is darkness, not light…" (Amos 5:18)* Amos' suggestion is that the Lord will bring darkness to those living in sin but light to the rest. God's righteousness came to mean judgment: condemnation rather than vindication.

We need to reclaim the understanding from Deborah's *Song of Deliverance*. Let us recapture the mood in which all are absolutely convinced of God putting all things right for his people. When we think of "The Day of the Lord" as a dire judgment day when bad people will get "their just desserts", we are turning ourselves into the judges. Martin Luther claimed that we are all simultaneously sinners and saints. One rabbinic tradition suggests that any separation of bad from good will be from within the hearts of every person.

You remember Jesus' statement (in John 12:31): *"**Now** is the judgment of this world" (emphasis mine)*. Well, guess what! God's justice is not **retribution** (an eye for an eye); we are not *"sinners in the hands of an angry God"**. God's justice is **distribution**. Blessings for all! And *"**The Day of the Lord**"*? It already happened…on Good Friday…once and for all. Thanks be to God! Amen.

"Then justice will dwell in the wilderness,
and righteousness abide in the fruitful field.

The effect of righteousness will be peace,
and the result of righteousness,
quietness and trust forever.
My people will abide in a peaceful habitation,
in secure dwellings, and in quiet resting places." Isaiah 32:16-18

*Jonathan Edwards, Sermon, 1741.

End-Note

"The days are surely coming, says the LORD, when I will make a new covenant with the house of Israel and the house of Judah. It will not be like the covenant that I made with their ancestors when I took them by the hand to bring them out of the land of Egypt—a covenant that they broke, though I was their husband, says the LORD. But this is the covenant that I will make with the house of Israel after those days, says the LORD: I will put my law within them, and I will write it on their hearts; and I will be their God, and they shall be my people. No longer shall they teach one another, or say to each other, 'Know the LORD,' for they shall all know me, from the least of them to the greatest, says the LORD; for I will forgive their iniquity, and remember their sin no more." Jeremiah 31:31-34

Bonus Feature:
A Calendar for Matching Essays to Days in Lent

Ash Wednesday—*In the Beginning*
Thursday after Ash Wednesday—*The Breath of Life*
Friday after Ash Wednesday—*In His Image*
Saturday after Ash Wednesday—*Subdue It*
First Sunday of Lent (Invocabit)—*What Have You Done?*
Week One Monday—*What Was the Original Sin?*
Week One Tuesday—*Torah! Torah! Torah!*
Week One Wednesday—*Toledoth*
Week One Thursday—*God's Memory*
Week One Friday—*Angelic Messengers*
Week One Saturday—*Ready, Willing & Able*
Second Sunday of Lent (Reminiscere)—*God's In His Heaven*
Week Two Monday—*What's In a Name?*
Week Two Tuesday—*Whom Do You Serve?*
Week Two Wednesday—*I Am Not a Man of Words*
Week Two Thursday—*Mountain Experiences*
Week Two Friday—*Guide Me, O Thou Great Jehovah*
Week Two Saturday—*Hardened Heart*
Third Sunday of Lent (Oculi)—*God Remembered*
Week Three Monday—*Forty Days*
Week Three Tuesday—*Sibling Rivalry*
Week Three Wednesday—*First-Fruits, Firstlings, Firstborn*
Week Three Thursday—*Covenantal Love*
Week Three Friday—*Jealous God*
Week Three Saturday—*Thirteen Attributes of Mercy*
Fourth Sunday of Lent (Laetare)—*The Crimson Cord*
Week Four Monday—*Bread from Heaven*
Week Four Tuesday—*The Big Ten*
Week Four Wednesday—*Tabernacling with God*
Week Four Thursday—*Mercy Seat*
Week Four Friday—*One That Bites*
Week Four Saturday—*Symbol of Seventy*
Fifth Sunday of Lent (Judica)—*Songs of Deliverance*
Week Five Monday—*The Glory of the Lord*
Week Five Tuesday—*Everlasting Covenant*
Week Five Wednesday—*Sabbath*
Week Five Thursday—*The Face of God*

111

Week Five Friday—*To Bless and to Curse*
Week Five Saturday—*To Judge or Not to Judge*
Sixth Sunday of Lent (Palmarum)/Palm Sunday—*My Redeemer*
Week Six Monday—*The Satan*
Week Six Tuesday—*The Anointed One*
Week Six Wednesday—*Proclaim Release to the Captives*
Maundy Thursday—*The Fourth Cup*
Good Friday—*One-Year-Old Lamb without Blemish*
Holy Saturday—*On the Third Day*
Easter Sunday—*The Righteous One*

Bonus Feature:
A Lenten Countdown of Blessings

Instructions: Here is a Lenten discipline with a family focus for increasing awareness and thanksgiving for blessings and an opportunity to give to others less fortunate. For each day, count the items indicated, then add that many coins to a special bank for your charitable project.

⌘Ash Wednesday⌘

How many sinks are in your home?

Give thanks for fresh water!

⌘Thursday after Ash Wednesday⌘

How many slices of bread are in your kitchen?

Give thanks for farmers who grow the wheat!

⌘Friday after Ash Wednesday⌘

How many pets do you have?

Give thanks for the companionship of God's creatures!

⌘Saturday after Ash Wednesday⌘

How many flashlights do you have?

Give thanks for light that shines in the darkness!

Continued

✠First Sunday in Lent✠
How many pews are in your church?
Give thanks for your church family!

✠Week One Monday✠
How many doors are in your home?
Give thanks for freedom!

✠Week One Tuesday✠
How many cans of vegetables are in your pantry?
Give thanks for markets!

✠Week One Wednesday✠
How many radios do you have?
Give thanks for inventions that keep us connected!

✠Week One Thursday✠
How many vitamins are in your house?
Give thanks for good health!

✠Week One Friday✠
How many sweaters do you have?
Give thanks for protection from bad weather!

✠Week One Saturday✠
How many Bibles are in your home?
Give thanks for the Word of God!

⌘Second Sunday in Lent⌘
How many crosses can you count in your church?
Give thanks for Jesus!

⌘Week Two Monday⌘
How many clocks are in your home?
Give thanks for time with family!

⌘Week Two Tuesday⌘
How many musical instruments are in your home?
Give thanks for the joy of music!

⌘Week Two Wednesday⌘
How many soap dispensers are in your home?
Give thanks for cleanliness!

⌘Week Two Thursday⌘
How many stop signs do you see today?
Give thanks for laws that keep us protected and safe!

⌘Week Two Friday⌘
How many bottles of water are in your kitchen?
Give thanks for fresh water to drink!

⌘Week Two Saturday⌘
How many tubes of toothpaste do you have?
Give thanks for teeth and our amazing bodies!

✠Third Sunday in Lent✠
How many churches did you go past today?
Give thanks for all God's churches!

✠Week Three Monday✠
How many mailboxes do you see from your driveway?
Give thanks for neighbors and community!

✠Week Three Tuesday✠
How many books are in your bedroom?
Give thanks for education!

✠Week Three Wednesday✠
How many trees are in your backyard?
Give thanks for the beauty of nature!

✠Week Three Thursday✠
How many beds are in your home?
Give thanks for the comforts of a home!

✠Week Three Friday✠
How many windows are in your home?
Give thanks for fresh air to breathe!

✠Week Three Saturday✠
How many words are in the Lord's Prayer?
Give thanks that God listens to our prayers!

✠Fourth Sunday in Lent✠
How many songs are sung in church today?
Give thanks for music in worship!

✠Week Four Monday✠
How many cans of soup in your kitchen?
Give thanks for all our food!

✠Week Four Tuesday✠
How many aspirin tablets are in your home?
Give thanks for doctors and nurses!

✠Week Four Wednesday✠
How many electrical outlets are in your home?
Give thanks for the convenience of electricity!

✠Week Four Thursday✠
How many sunglasses do you own?
Give thanks of the gift of sunshine!

✠Week Four Friday✠
How many cousins do you have?
Give thanks for the gift of family!

✠Week Four Saturday✠
How many heating vents are in your home?
Give thanks for warmth and shelter!

✠Fifth Sunday in Lent✠
How many "amens" do you hear this morning?
Give thanks that God hears us!

✠Week Five Monday✠
How many band-aids are in your home?
Give thanks for health care!

✠Week Five Tuesday✠
How many candles are in your home?
Give thanks for the gift of light!

✠Week Five Wednesday✠
How many umbrellas are in your home?
Give thanks for the gift of rain to make things grow!

✠Week Five Thursday✠
How many tires are on your cars or bikes?
Give thanks for the gift of transportation!

✠Week Five Friday✠
How many telephones and cell phones do you have?
Give thanks for the gift of language!

✠Week Five Saturday✠
How many toilets are in your home?
Give thanks for indoor plumbing!

⌘Palm Sunday⌘
How many people are in the choir?
Give thanks for music in worship!

⌘Week Six Monday⌘
How many pieces of fruit are in your kitchen?
Give thanks for the food God provides!

⌘Week Six Tuesday⌘
How many houseplants are in your home?
Give thanks for the gift of every green plant in nature!

⌘Week Six Wednesday⌘
How many words are in the song "Jesus Loves Me"?
Give thanks for Jesus!

⌘Maundy Thursday⌘
How many people can you tell "I love you"?
Give thanks for the people who love you!

⌘Good Friday⌘
How many eggs are in your refrigerator?
Give thanks for all farm animals!

⌘Holy Saturday⌘
How many boxes of cereal are in your kitchen?
Give thanks for the gift of nutritious food!

⌘Easter Sunday⌘
How many "alleluias" do you hear today?
Give thanks for Easter!

Count your coins and make your donation!

Index of Scriptural References

Genesis

Index of Vocabulary

❖ **A** ❖

abad, 17, 39
Accuser, 93
adam, 11
adamah, 11
adonai, 45
Adversary, 93
Amidah, 95
angel, 29
angelos, 29
anointed, 95
Ark of the Covenant, 71
atonement, 71

❖ **B** ❖

barak, 87
barren woman, 27
benedictions, 88
berit, 81
berit olam, 81
bless, 87
b-kor, 55
bread from heaven, 65
breath of life, 13

❖ **C** ❖

canticle, 77
charis, 57
cherubim, 71
Christos, 95
commandments, 59, 68
countenance, 85

covenant, 57, 81
created light, 34
crimson cord, 63
curse, 19, 87

❖ **D** ❖
Day of the Lord, 108
Decalogue, 41, 83
deliver, 89
Deuteronomist, 67
dominium, 18
dominion, 18
doxa, 80

❖ **E** ❖
-el, 37
Eloist, 67
empyrean, 34
eskenosen, 70

❖ **F** ❖
face, 85
Festival of Booths, 103
Festival of Dedication, 103
Festival of Lights, 103
Festival of Weeks, 102
firstborn, 55
first-fruits, 55
firstlings, 55
forty, 51
four, 51, 75

❖ X-Y ❖

❖ Z ❖

Helpful Resources

The Analytical Concordance to the New Revised Standard Version of the New Testament by Richard W. Whitaker and John R. Kohlenberger III, Oxford University Press, 2000.

Berit Olam: Studies in Hebrew Narrative and Poetry by David W. Cotter, Liturgical Press, Minnesota, 2003.

The Bible with Sources Revealed by Richard Elliot Friedman, Harper San Francisco, 2003.

Discovering Old Testament Origins by Margaret Nutting Ralph, Wipf and Stock Publishers, 1992.

A Father Who Keeps His Promises by Scott Hahn, Servant Books, Ohio, 1998.

God's Secretaries by Adam Nicolson, Harper Collins Publishers, 2003.

The Harper Collins Bible Dictionary by Paul J. Achtemeier, General Editor, The Easton Press, 2005.

The Harper Collins Study Bible (New Revised Standard Version) by Wayne A. Meeks, General Editor, Harper Collins Publishers, 1993.

Hidden Voices by Heidi Bright Parales, Smyth & Helwys Publishing, Inc., 1998.

In Memory of Her by Elisabeth Schüssler Fiorenza, Crossroad, 1998.

The Jewish Holidays by Michael Strassfield, William Morrow, 1985.

The Jewish Study Bible (TANAKH translation), Jewish Publication Society, Oxford University Press, 2004.

The Literary Structure of the Old Testament by David A. Dorsey, Baker Books, Michigan, 1999.

136

The New Oxford Annotated Bible (New Revised Standard Version), Third Edition, Michael D. Cogan, Editor, Oxford University Press, 2001.

The NRSV Concordance Unabridged by John R. Kohlenberger III, Zondervan Publishing House, 1991.

The Oxford Bible Commentary, edited by J. Barton and J. Muddiman, Oxford University Press, 2001.

The Road to Redemption by Rabbi Burt Visotzky, Crown Publishers, 1998.

Vine's Complete Expository Dictionary of Old and New Testament Words, W. E. Vine; Merril F. Unger; William White, Jr.; Thomas Nelson Publishers, 1985.

Vine's Expository Dictionary of Old & New Testament Words, W. E. Vine, Thomas Nelson Publishers, 1997.